PRAISE FOR
SO HERE'S THE THING…

"Reading SO HERE'S THE THING…is exactly like hanging out with Alyssa. You will laugh a lot, learn even more, and just be grateful that she is your friend."
—Dan Pfeiffer, #1 *New York Times* bestselling author of *Yes We (Still) Can* and cohost of *Pod Save America*

"My favorite thing about Alyssa's books is knowing someone as normal as the rest of us can work in the most prestigious positions in the world and do it with a sense of humor and self-deprecation. We could all do with more of both. Read it, and laugh."
—Chelsea Handler, #1 *New York Times* bestselling author of *Are You There, Vodka? It's Me, Chelsea*

"Growing up is hard. Trusting your gut? Sheesh. That sounds impossible at times. Let Alyssa Mastromonaco hold your hand and show you that with some good laughs and a lot of heart, life can be a little less daunting. I wish I'd read this book when I was younger, but it still resonates today, and I know it will be relevant at all stages of life. What a gift."
—Aminatou Sow, co-founder of Tech LadyMafia

"I'm just going to say this book lets the 'cat out of the bag,' so to speak: Everyone who knows her or reads her work wants to be Alyssa's best friend. SO HERE'S THE THING...makes it impossible not to want that. Her life stories somehow make all of us feel seen. All of which means my position on the waiting list for the best friend title may shift. While I'm coming to terms with that, I will also say I'm all for mixing patterns, just not always the ones Alyssa puts together."

—Stacy London, *New York Times* bestselling author of
The Truth About Style

"[SO HERE'S THE THING...] is a delightful, digestible nosh of useful tips from Mastromonaco's long career in politics."

—*Portland Mercury*

"Funny and...insightful. An entertaining miscellany by a sharp-eyed observer."

—*Kirkus*

"Behind-the-scenes moments from [Mastromonaco's] career provide insights into the hectic work of campaigns and the White House...readers will enjoy the relaxed tone that Mastromonaco and co-author Oyler set throughout—like chatting with old friend, who just happened to have Mindy Kaling set up her Twitter account."

—*Booklist*

So Here's the Thing...

ALSO BY ALYSSA MASTROMONACO

Who Thought This Was a Good Idea?: And Other Questions You Should Have Answers to When You Work in the White House

So Here's the Thing...

Notes on Growing Up, Getting Older, and Trusting Your Gut

Alyssa Mastromonaco
with Lauren Oyler

TWELVE

New York Boston

Twelve
Hachette Book Group
1290 Avenue of the Americas, New York, NY 10104
twelvebooks.com
twitter.com/twelvebooks

Originally published in hardcover and ebook by Twelve in March 2019.

First Trade Edition: March 2020

Twelve is an imprint of Grand Central Publishing. The Twelve name and logo
are trademarks of Hachette Book Group, Inc.

The publisher is not responsible for websites (or their content) that are not
owned by the publisher.

The Hachette Speakers Bureau provides a wide range of authors for speaking
events. To find out more, go to www.hachettespeakersbureau.com or call (866)
376-6591.

Photo on page 227 courtesy of the author.

Library of Congress Control Number: 2018963133

ISBNs: 978-1-5387-3156-7 (trade pbk.), 978-1-5387-3154-3 (ebook)

Printed in the United States of America

LSC-C

10 9 8 7 6 5 4 3 2 1

This one is for all the wee dames-in-training:
JJ (aka "Cheeks"), Alice, Gigi, Val, Hailey, Lilz,
Emily, Freddie, Nina, Ruby, Nico, Emzy,
Grace, Sofia, Kyla, Clara—and Midge!

Contents

Contents

Once in a while you get shown the light
in the strangest of places if you look at it right.

"Scarlet Begonias," Grateful Dead

Introduction

People these days want to make definitive statements, and to read definitive statements. Chalk it up to the political situation, which is confusing, unpredictable, and destabilizing—everyone wants something solid and dependable to latch on to. They want the comfort and clarity of advice to steady them during these wild times.

Unfortunately, I believe the best advice is not definitive but situational. That's what I like about the phrase "So here's the thing." Which I happen to say all the time. I mean, *all* the time. When people ask me for advice, I understand they want something straightforward, an injunction: "Do this, and everything will be fine!" But I don't work that way. I want to help my friends and colleagues—and the occasional Twitter user who @'s me—weigh options and then pick the best one, considering all the benefits and drawbacks, without denial or wishful thinking.

So here's the thing (sorry, I had to): I think this is a good attitude to bring to writing a book, which is all about exploration, not declaration. In my first book, *Who Thought This Was a Good Idea?*, I wanted to suggest that everyone is different and that there's no right path or way to deal with a problem or achieve a goal. Here's the cheesy, oversimplified synopsis, for the purposes of this introduction: I used myself as an example of how, though I had only a vague idea of where I wanted to go, flexibility and adaptability helped me accomplish everything I did, which includes becoming the White House deputy chief of staff for operations for President Barack Obama. These qualities—flexibility and adaptability— are realistic ones. They require you to think about a particular set of circumstances and respond to them accordingly.

I didn't really start thinking in terms of "so here's the thing" until the summer of 2008. Before Obama became the Democratic presidential nominee, we'd been talking about taking a foreign trip as part of the campaign. As a candidate, you're not given any resources for foreign travel, so all the transport, logistics, security, and everything else would be totally on us. The idea was to go to two or three countries to showcase Obama's diplomacy skills, get some good press for being capable and charming abroad, and generally demonstrate how popular he'd be around the world. All fun in theory, but always very distant in practice. We had mostly tried not to get our hopes up about Obama getting nominated at all because it seemed like such a long shot.

But then of course he did become the nominee, so we had to have a real talk about the foreign trip. A conference call was scheduled. I dialed in on time, but when I got there, it seemed everyone else was already talking passionately. The call was under way. And soon my life was flashing before my eyes. The number of countries being mentioned was not two or three. Jordan. Israel. France. The UK. Germany. It was as if they had purposefully arranged to start the call earlier so the decision could be made before I got on. I was the director of scheduling and advance, so planning this was going to be on me.

But as the excited conversation progressed, I couldn't say no. I would never say no. I don't think that's how you get what you want, and anyway, I'm always willing to be wrong. Except when it comes to other people's love lives. I have 100 percent accuracy on that.

So instead of saying no [way in hell are we doing five countries], I said something to the effect of, "So here's the thing: I think three countries is achievable—we can execute that. But five is a no-can-do."

This did not get me the result I wanted. But it did inspire a long conversation in which my fears were moderately assuaged, or I was forced to admit that the cost-benefit analysis did not add up in my favor. Yeah, we did five. And it worked so well because every step of the way, we were being realistic about what we could and could not accomplish. Since "so here's the thing" is also a gentle (probably feminine) way of letting people know they might not like what you're about to say, it's also helpful when you're handing out undesirable assignments. When we were thinking about how we would coordinate logistics back home when we were traversing so many different time zones and continuing to plan parts of the trip (meaning:

When we were in Israel, there was still a lot of Germany to sort out), I remember telling the team who would be in the States, "So here's the thing: We're basically going to need twenty-four-hour coverage, so you guys are going to have to figure out what works best. I need to know who I can call when I need answers." (Translation: Someone was going to have to be manning—or womanning—the phones at 4:00 AM.) The tables were turned when a staff member for the company that owned the plane we were chartering from Amman to Tel Aviv began a sentence, "So here's the thing: The landing gear…" I really did not want to have to go to Obama and say, "So here's the thing: The plane won't fly." (Luckily, the landing gear turned out to be OK.)

This book is an attempt at a conversation, not a statement. It's *the thing*. What you learn as time goes on is that nothing is perfect, and there's always a *the thing*. "So here's the thing" means I'm basically about to edit something you're thinking or doing, in the nicest way possible. It might be about needing to break up with a boyfriend, quit a job, apply for a higher-level position, or figure out a way to pay off your student loans, but there's always *the thing*. It's gotten to the point where my starting a sentence with "So here's the thing" sends everyone at work into a frenzy.

"Oh no!" they cry. "Not *the thing*!"

WTF Is Politics Anymore?

As an experiment, I'm going to list, off the top of my head, all the news I can remember interrupting me while I was trying to write this book:

- Students organized a nationwide walkout to protest gun violence.
- Donald Trump pulled out of the Iran nuclear deal.
- It was revealed that ICE had been separating migrant children from their parents at the border and detaining them without keeping track of who they were or how their parents could be reached.
- Trump treated his historic summit with North Korea like a WWE match-up, alternately trading insults and boasting so that no one knew if it would actually happen.
- John McCain died.
- An anonymous senior staffer in the Trump administration published an op-ed in the *New York Times* claiming

there was a "shadow Cabinet" specifically dedicated to undermining Trump's leadership. ("Leadership.")

- Brett Kavanaugh, Trump's nominee for the Supreme Court, was accused of sexual harassment by Dr. Christine Blasey Ford, ushering in a slew of further accusations against him. Dr. Blasey Ford and Kavanaugh testified in front of the Senate Judiciary Committee, an occasion that involved the latter saying things like "I like drinking beer" as evidence of his suitability to be confirmed.

- He was, despite the ludicrousness of the affair and the unanimous agreement that Dr. Blasey Ford's testimony was credible, confirmed to the Supreme Court.

- The *New York Times* published an article claiming that Rod Rosenstein suggested secretly recording Trump in order to gather evidence for invoking the Twenty-Fifth Amendment.

- The long-awaited midterm Blue Wave maybe happened? It's unclear. The Democrats regained control of the House by the biggest margin since Watergate, but the GOP retained control of the Senate, as was expected. Reports of rampant voter suppression inspired outrage, and several races remained too close to call for weeks.

It wasn't all bad. I woke up at 6:00 AM to watch the Royal Wedding with enthusiasm (and themed snacks). Ireland overturned its abortion ban. But the overall impression has been one of shock, followed by the sense that I shouldn't still be shocked at this point. Repeat. Trump is doing exactly what he said he would, and then some, which is what he suggested he would do. Yet scrolling through Twitter still feels like an emotional roller coaster, one of the old, rickety wooden ones you're pretty sure would never pass a safety inspection today: Anything funny or lighthearted is inevitably followed by some breaking *New York Times* investigation that reveals everything to be worse than you imagined. You leave feeling shaky, disoriented, and like you're definitely going to hurt tomorrow.

It's a privilege to be shocked: I understand that as a middle-aged white woman with money, I have always been and will always be insulated from the real effects of these policies. I'm not going to be needing an abortion anytime soon (and if I did, I could easily access one). But I also think it's important to be honest about where we're all coming from if we're going to build a viable resistance and, eventually, win back the White House. Because from where I sit, the left remains a hot mess.

When my first book came out in March 2017, the reality of the Trump presidency had not really sunk in. I'd expected to unleash the book into an atmosphere of hope and optimism brought in by the first female president, who would, I expected, more or less continue Obama's policies. When I woke up to my tear-stained pillow on November 9, 2016, to confirm that the Trump thing wasn't just a nightmare, I realized, too, that I had no idea what was actually going to happen. It just seemed like a huge cloud of BAD was about to descend on my former workplace.

Now, more than two years later, I still quite frankly have

no idea what's going to happen. Or what's happening now. As someone who had a long, successful career working in government, and who is now regularly called upon to comment on politics, I'm supposed to be an expert on it. But the only thing I can say from experience is that trying to predict what will come of Trump's volatility and wake of destruction is a waste of time. I can tell you what it means that Trump didn't visit Canada until more than a year after he took office and hasn't yet been to Mexico at all. I can tell you what it means that he hadn't filled hundreds of government positions more than five hundred days after he took office. I can tell you what the chief of staff does and why it was gravely concerning that Trump's first one resigned in disgrace—remember that? It's like it happened decades ago—and that his second one probably told Bob Woodward that the president is "an idiot."

But what's going to happen? Trying to answer that question is an exercise in futility that only makes well-meaning pundits look like out-of-touch know-it-alls. The Republicans can't even predict what Trump's going to do or what scandalous cover-up is going to come out, and they're totally desperate to do so in order to maintain their status as ringleaders of the circus. I have to admit, it is a little fun to watch Mitch McConnell and John Kelly scramble to clarify or retract whatever inane thing Trump has said or done. But it's not that fun, because it makes clear that nothing in the American government matters if no one believes it does.

This is an uncool position to take, but the revelation that institutions like the presidency might be held together

by little more than the Tinkerbell effect was deeply disappointing to me. When I go on TV to comment on
something, I sometimes feel like I'm screaming "BUT IT'S
IMPORTANT!" into a void. Maybe it's that I don't want
all the work I've done over the years to be for nothing.
It's partially that. But it's also true that I did all that work
because I believed that I was helping, in some small way,
to make people's lives easier. I believed things were slowly
but surely getting better.

◆ ◆ ◆

I have a memory of being woken up at 5:15 in the morning
by Rahm Emanuel back in 2006 that I think illustrates how
much things have changed. I was working for Obama, who
was, like many popular sitting senators, on the campaign trail
for the midterm elections, boosting Democratic candidates.

I was also hooking up with a guy named Bob. His house
always smelled like mildew. We had gotten wasted the night
before, so when my phone rang at 5:15 AM, I considered
letting it go. I was desperately hungover. But I knew we were
in a high-stakes moment, and when I looked at the caller ID
I saw that it was Rahm, who was the head of the Democratic
Congressional Campaign Committee (DCCC) at the time.

"Alyssa. Alyssa? It's Rahm, Rahm. It's Rahm. Alyssa.
John? John's dead. He's not going to be able to do anything else. He's radioactive. He really fucked up. He really
fucked me over."

Because my brain was wading through alcohol, I groggily

assumed for a second he meant that John—as in Kerry—was literally dead. But no. What he meant was that John Kerry was supposed to campaign for a string of top-tier candidates for the promised Blue Wave in November, but the night before he had committed a gaffe: He'd said students who can't navigate America's education system risked "get[ting] stuck in Iraq." Fox News and Republicans were already having a field day: John Kerry thought *soldiers*—our *TROOPS!*—were *stupid*.

Rahm was still on the phone. "John's out, honey. He can't go on. I gotta fill all these targets. Here's what I need, all right…"

I got out of bed. (Far from being miffed that his lover was abandoning him in the middle of the cold, dark night, Bob was seriously impressed that I was fielding calls from Rahm Emanuel at five in the morning.) I told Rahm that Obama could replace Kerry at several events, went to Dunkin' Donuts for a coffee, and prepared to inform Obama of his new schedule. Obama was annoyed—I believe the comment was: "Are you working for Rahm or me?"—but Obama's involvement during that campaign season also catapulted him from promising young senator to "That guy should really run for president." And the thing was, we all knew Rahm wasn't wrong. John Kerry *was* radioactive and wouldn't have been any help to anyone. He'd also been planning to run for president again in 2008, but his glib remark meant he'd no longer be able to.

The fact that one ungenerously interpreted offhand comment could ruin John Kerry's hopes of running for president again was not an indication that the American political system was healthy. No. Particularly because he *wasn't* insulting the military. He was making a basic yet important point: America needed to invest more in education so that young people from lower-class backgrounds didn't feel the military was their only option. Any normal person would be able to see he wasn't disparaging the military. It didn't matter.

But if traditionally politics was guided by oversensitivity, today it's guided by blatant, shameless opportunism. There's been a total 180. Whereas every single comment used to be dissected with ruthless bad faith, now nothing anyone says matters at all. How many times has some news story broken to cries of "This is finally the nail in the coffin for Trump"? And it never is.

◆ ◆ ◆

How are we, as engaged citizens, supposed to react to the news? There's a confusing disconnect between the experience of reading the news (whiplash) and the apparent lack of effect it has on the actual political situation (Trump is still in office). On one hand, it's critically important that we not get complacent and start treating the cruel absurdity as "normal." On the other, despite our best efforts, the news cycle is becoming normal—the outrage that follows any one abysmal policy decision is drowned out by the outrage that follows the next one. Democratic presidential hopefuls tweet grave rebukes of the Trump administration to much celebration on social media and little practical avail. Republicans get aggravated, pay lip service to their constituents' furious concerns, and then ultimately do exactly what they planned on doing in the first place. Everyone in government seems more concerned with their images than with the clusterfuck they've wrought on the American people.

This has effects both in America and around the world. In 2014, Obama was the first sitting president to visit Burma, to encourage the country's liberalization process after the relative easing of its military regime. Though the optimism of that visit took a turn shortly after, going on that trip was a reminder of how much significance the American president has around the world, not just to diplomats and leaders but to ordinary people. There were so many people in the streets, waving Burmese and American flags, that they couldn't be held back; the motorcade was going at parade speed—with POTUS still freaking out about hitting someone. Even if the policy discussion was flawed, the effect his visit had on the Burmese people was clear: He was validating them. Of course, a visit from an American president shouldn't be a validating event for an entire nation. American foreign policy has often been ruthless and terrible. But that's the world we live in, and seeing the happiness Obama brought those people was something of a consolation.

Maybe it was always a house of cards. (I guess that's why the show is called *House of Cards*.) But I think there was some value in it. By treating foreign governments and peoples as though they're pawns to be manipulated in a game that

America is rigged to win, Trump is insulting them. Even the way the administration communicates with the people is ad hoc and panic-inducing. For months, the appearance of a new Trump tweet on North Korea would be followed by strings of semiserious text messages from friends asking if there's a fallout shelter near my house and saying that if the world is going to end at least I won't have to go on my business trip next week. Trump often brags about having avoided war with North Korea—forgetting, I guess, that his ability to do so is thanks to all the previous presidents, who also avoided war with North Korea. And they did it without so fully terrorizing the citizens of both countries. You can see that people are scared. It's not as if other presidents haven't engaged in brinkmanship, or high-flown back-and-forths, but they haven't done so with the volatile intensity of Trump's tweets, which foment panic and urgency. What's more, the way Trump teased the Kim Jong-un summit, as if it were the season finale of a reality TV show, frittered away the significance of the diplomatic opportunity. Who-ever comes after Trump—if anyone does—is going to have a very difficult task ahead of them if they want to restore the meaning of those kinds of visits and of the American government in general.

Of course, political rhetoric has always been strategic and biased. The difference is that in the past, politicians might have made statements you disagreed with, in order to sway voters. Obviously, you're always going to present an issue the way you see it. But there's a difference between Obama saying "The ACA is going to help many families stay out of poverty by giving them access to basic health care" and, as Trump once tweeted, "Obamacare is imploding. It is a disaster and 2017 will be the worst year yet, by far!" For the people who depend on Obamacare for health insurance, that kind of fear-mongering has a real effect. By treating every issue with the same level of intensity and hostility, Trump is a propaganda machine, sowing anxiety in order to scare his base into voting for him. When most presidents get into office, they make an attempt to speak to the entire American population, to at least gesture toward bipartisanship. The Democrats have been too conciliatory in this way. But Trump communicates as the Republican president to his core MAGA supporters and seems to truly believe that everyone else is out to get him. He is incapable of taking his own power into account or of understanding any actual policies. He never explains his own position (probably because he doesn't really have one) and instead just says whatever he wants at the time. He has no sense of responsibility to anyone but himself.

I wish I could say that I felt confident in our side's ability to respond to all this. But I can't say that. It sometimes seems as if the Democratic Party is engaged in a slapstick performance of ineptitude for laughs. There's no other way to explain why they do some of the things they do. Nobody is ever going to beat Donald Trump playing his game. When Chuck Schumer or Nancy Pelosi tries to be as inflammatory as Trump, it just lands flat; they can't rouse people, and worse, the obviousness of their attempts to rouse people makes them look worse. (If you're going to try, you need to make it your own!) Donald Trump is a television producer, desperate for ratings and an expert at getting them; the people who are up against him are legislators who look ridiculous when they act as though they're auditioning for roles on a reality TV show about American politics.

While I was working on this book, people kept talking about Joe Biden as a top candidate for 2020. Joe Biden. Joe Biden! I love, love, love Joe Biden. But pollsters and pundits, desperate for someone to root for, get dazzled by name recognition and put him at 30 to 40 percent odds, forgetting that most of America has never heard of Kamala Harris, Cory Booker, or Kirsten Gillibrand. Eric Gar-who? The 2020 field is going to be absolutely packed. Anything could happen. Joe Biden polls high not because Americans *want* Joe Biden but because he's the best person they've heard of.

I always have to think long and hard about how to disagree with Democrats because I'm afraid I'll get kicked out of the party. Which is part of the problem. The left's mantra is supposed to be about inclusivity, but you only get included if you have the same views the algorithm came up with. Those at the top of the DNC don't want to listen to any criticism or consider any viewpoint that doesn't mesh with their vision for the party, which is based way too much on appearances and not enough on grunt work and boots on the ground. Even after the 2016 election—when I told them, screaming into the void, "Pay attention to Bernie!"— some members of the party still refuse to see what's right in front of their faces. Back in 1994, "progressive" was code for "socialist"; now it means a non-moderate Democrat, someone who's on the right track but not fully on board with the agenda many young people want, which includes Medicare for all, free tuition, and criminal justice reform. Even for me, someone who is basically a socialist—does this count as my coming out?—it's still surreal to see the label being proudly embraced by millennials, Gen Z, and even politicians. But I'll get used to it, and the Democrats need to, too. People want government health care. People want dignity and expanded social services. People are sick of seeing downright villains get away unscathed from the wreckage they've caused and with their riches intact. It's a shame that the next Democrat to win the presidency is going to have to fight his or her own party for legitimacy. Whoever does it will have to run without fear of losing and without backing from the polls.

Maybe by the time you read this we'll have a better sense of who the Democrats will run. Regardless, I don't look forward to watching the overcrowded primary debates. As voters, we have a responsibility to start looking at who really wants it—not who wants it because they want to be the president, because they want to see themselves in that office (and with that Twitter handle) but because they want to serve. The election in 2016 showed us that polls are not a reliable foundation on which to build a campaign. The people are. The best politicians, the ones I get excited about, know that.

◆　◆　◆

When I left the White House, I wanted to be done with it all. I was tired. I'm conflict-averse, and I felt I'd done my time. I don't like the sparring and politicking and behind-the-scenes jousting. I hated the theater of the dueling press releases, and I hate the spectacle of Twitter even more.

And never did I imagine that two and a half years after leaving my office in the West Wing—a building I didn't just respect but loved with my whole heart—I would be outside those gates protesting a new president who gloated about grabbing pussies. On the one hand, it would be easy for me to tap out and avoid involvement.

On the other, I couldn't do that in good conscience.

It's not like I think my participation in politics is necessary or meaningful. Nobody's is. But I worked too hard, and saw too much, to sit idly by as a bigot reigns over the Oval Office. The only way to make an impact is as a collective, which we can't form if everyone is bickering over strategy and focus. It can be difficult to figure out what to do, how to get involved, when there are so many problems and they all seem impossible to fix and you're just one person sitting at your computer reading the news. But like it or not, you probably already know what you can do to get involved. It starts with being really, truly engaged with what's happening and how different politicians are proposing to respond to it. The best way to help get us out of this mess is by voting and by vocally supporting candidates who seem authentically dedicated to fighting for policies you want—not just for their own glory. After that, doing work for organizations that focus on causes you care about, donating money to those groups and to campaigns, and volunteering to knock on doors or phone-bank for campaigns are all not at all pointless ways to fight for change. The main point is that you can't tweet the resistance. You have to join it.

SUSAN RICE ON HOW DIPLOMACY HAS CHANGED (AND HOW YOUNG WOMEN CAN HELP SHAPE IT)

Though most people will know the formidable Susan Rice. as the former national security advisor for Barack Obama, ambassador to the UN, and staff member of the National Security Council and assistant secretary of state for African Affairs under Bill Clinton, I know her as all those things and as an awesome dancer. One of my favorite memories of working with Susan was from the "Last Chance Dance Vajamboree," a going-away party Kathy Ruemmler and I held when we left the White House. Susan's moves were so inspired that when Mindy Kaling walked into the room, she said, "Oh my God—is that the national security advisor dropping it like it's hot?!"

It was. Though I don't expect Susan to reveal the secrets to her success on the dance floor in my book, she was gracious enough to share some insight into her career and into politics right now.

You served in the Clinton administration, before Al Gore invented the internet, and then in the Obama administration, when we all had to learn what Twitter was. How do you think social media has changed the way we govern—for better or worse?

There have been two major changes in the media since I began as a twenty-eight-year-old staffer in President Clinton's

NSC *in early 1993. First, we have gone from the three original TV networks (ABC, NBC, CBS) plus CNN to tons of twenty-four-hour cable options, and from major, big-city print newspapers to all kinds of online news offerings. Second, we have seen the advent of social media.*

Together, these trends have vastly changed the landscape for governing and policy-making. The pace of information flow is infinitely faster, so people in power have to respond to events instantaneously and often without ample time for thoughtful consideration of various courses of action. In addition, with social media, consumers can pick and choose their own sources of information—and even what they wish to be their own "facts." We no longer have a baseline (like Walter Cronkite) telling us what is happening. Without common information and a real, agreed factual basis for decision-making, Americans are talking past one another, and the quality and utility of public debate is greatly diminished. Civil discourse is under attack, starting from the Oval Office, and the fabric of our society is fraying. I believe these developments pose a potential long-term risk to the viability of our democracy.

On the positive side, social media has made information more readily accessible, galvanized collaborative efforts among users (for better and worse), and given informed consumers wider access to knowledge.

Bottom line: It was a lot easier to govern in the old days than it is today.

President Trump is constantly committing unbelievable diplomatic errors. Do you think it will be possible to restore the United States' diplomatic relationships once he leaves office? How will whoever is in office have to approach that task?

Every day President Trump is in office, he does more damage to America's ability to remain a global leader, much less a moral leader. The damage is almost incalculable. If he wins a second term, I think all bets are off.

If he is defeated, we have the chance to begin the long, difficult process of trying to regain international trust and respect. It will take a strong, principled, and visionary leader who understands the stakes to do so. He or she will need to persuade the world that the last four years were an aberration and that America is back and wants to earn the world's respect again. I think we can do it if we elect the right leader with real international knowledge and experience, but even for the best successor, it will be very challenging.

When we went to the Vatican together, I remember you were not stoked to wear the mantilla. Why? When you're traveling, how do you show respect for other cultures while being true to your values?

Truthfully, I am not keen on having to wear religiously mandated garb of any sort or to cover myself in a manner reserved for women. That's just my personal view. But as a diplomat, I understand the necessity of showing respect for other cultures and faiths. So I suck it up and wear it when I must but avoid it when I can. I did it at the Vatican and have worn a loose scarf around part of my head when necessary in certain mosques. But I don't have to be happy about it.

What advice would you give to young women who want to work in foreign service?

First of all, I strongly encourage young women to go into public service generally, and the foreign service in particular. Our nation needs its best talent to serve the greater good, and working in key roles in government can be extremely rewarding and important.

Second, you need to be well-prepared. Get an advanced degree (at least a master's, if you can). Travel abroad. Learn one or more foreign languages. Get some quantitative skills. Consider joining the Peace Corps. Test your limits, stretch yourself, get out of your comfort zone.

Finally, do what you are passionate about—not what your parents or your teachers or anyone else wants you to do. Do what will make you get out of bed in the morning with pep in your step. And try to find somebody worthy to share the journey with you.

Good luck, and have fun!

Shits, Giggles, and Medical Marijuana

Rule #1 of publishing a book: Never read the Amazon reviews. Even when they're pretty good—average 4.1 stars!!!—looking at them is a drag. Everyone knows that you need twenty enthusiastic compliments to counteract the force of one slightly, possibly passive-aggressive mention of the bad hair decision you made when you were twenty-three, and that's under ideal circumstances. Amazon reviewers tend to be less generous than your aunt Glenda at Thanksgiving, who seems to think your beauty never quite recovered from that perm.

So, before you lecture me on what's good for my mental health, I just want to say I know. But on the scale of difficult things, avoiding Amazon reviews of a book you've written falls somewhere between "not eating the entire pint of Ben & Jerry's in one sitting" and quantum physics. It requires the willpower of one of those really austere kinds of monks. Instead of a vow of silence, you have taken a vow not to type your own name into your search bar. Maybe it'll be different for this book, like how parents are progressively less involved with each subsequent kid. Book one gets obsessive Amazon scanning, book two gets the occasional update on rankings, book three just gets hand-me-downs. Mom's busy watching Netflix!

The main thing I've taken away from reading Amazon reviews that I shouldn't have read is that, for some reason, not everyone wants to hear about my unpredictable bowel movements. They were the pesky villains of my previous book, popping up when I least expected them to thwart my plans of dazzling the pope.

"We came here for gossip about whether Barack Obama still smokes sometimes," the Amazon reviewers cried, "not for endless anecdotes about some random lady's IBS!"

"Gross!"

"#TMI!"

All fair points. But would these readers be singing a different tune if they learned that being open about my struggle had earned me an invitation to speak at the 2017 IBS Awareness Summit in New York hosted by Wendy Williams?!

Probably not. Pooping—yes, I said it—is one of the last major taboos in our culture, and as with all taboos, that goes double for women, so people will probably be freaking out about it for a long time. As a woman, and one who has held various positions of power that are seen as serious and important, I thought of my discussion of my overactive intestines as a way to help lessen that stigma. (For every commenter noting how unladylike it is to discuss one's bowel movements, I would get a DM or email thanking me for talking about it.) I would rather not have to use the bathroom at all, but here we are. Maybe when the human race has fully transitioned into AI we'll be able to phase out shitting.

All this is to say: I'm about to talk about my IBS again! In much more detail than before. So if you're one of these reviewers, or someone who doesn't appreciate knowing the details of strangers' gastrointestinal lives (weird...), I suggest you skip to the next essay, which is about the much less gross topic of periods.

◆ ◆ ◆

I've always had a finicky stomach, but things really became noticeable on the Kerry campaign in 2004. I was dating Doug,[1] who also worked on the campaign and whom I'd been with for a few years. (Just so you know I'm not talking about diarrhea with some random hookup—I always saved that until at least date four.) Whenever I'd go on the road with Kerry, I'd talk to Doug about how bad my stomach was acting—like it was somehow separate from me. Doug would always say the same thing—that what I was describing was not normal, that I should go to the doctor—and I would always reply with the same thing: "No, no, I think I'm just lactose intolerant!" You'd think that when swapping milk with Lactaid had no

---

1   Not his real name.

effect on the number of panicked trips I took to the bathroom I would have realized dairy was not my problem, but no. So in addition to drinking Lactaid like the company had sponsored me on Instagram (before Instagram existed) I chugged Pepto-Bismol and popped Imodium, which just gave me the opposite problem at about the same intensity. I had great health insurance, but I kept putting off going to the doctor because I didn't want to have *a disease*—and particularly a disease that might make you shit your pants in front of friends, colleagues, and international luminaries.

Five years later—yes, five years—we got to the White House, and there was a tipping point. (I'll spare you the diarrhea pun I came up with.) While my job had always been stressful—you could describe it as absorbing some of the stress from Obama—nothing could have really prepared me for having to be on call 24/7 on behalf of, basically, the entire country. Smoking weed had always helped me deal with my symptoms, which are often brought on by stress, but I couldn't do that while I worked for the president, and the job was also much more hectic and, thus, even more inconvenient in terms of emergency bathroom access. I could take Xanax to deal with my anxiety occasionally, but it wasn't good for me to take it every day. And when I would inevitably get anxious, I would immediately think, *Shit*, which made me even more anxious. It was a vicious cycle, not unlike my digestion.

My visit to the doctor was pretty straightforward: a series of questions about what triggered my issues and then, "Yep, you have IBS." The confirmation was all I got, really; there's nothing you can do about it except to identify and limit your triggers. It was both edifying and disappointing; being able to point to a word and say "Yes, this is what I have" was more of a relief than I anticipated when I was freaking out about having *a disease*, but I also felt like I was being sentenced to something.

We came up with a plan for dealing with it, a whole multi-pronged attack. In addition to avoiding my trigger foods—eggs are a big one—I had to figure out how to limit my anxiety. The more prepared I was, the less anxiety I had, and although I've always been a notorious planner, I had to get more serious about preparation than a Boy Scout taking the LSAT. Though I don't think you need to have IBS to understand and implement the joys of lists in your life, the condition does provide a certain sense of urgency.

For starters, I stuck to a strict daily schedule that began with waking up super early to have coffee so I had enough time before I left the house to…take care of it. Breakfast was plain, basic—I won't say *boring*—food: muesli and a little English muffin. My gigantic purse also got a little heavier. I started bringing Imodium, Gas-X, ginger chews, and ginger ale with me everywhere.

I know this sounds very responsible and well-adjusted, but the feeling that there was no way I could get out of this easily made me frustrated and rebellious at times, too. Controlling my IBS requires following so many rules, and the condition affects everything; it's really hard to lose weight, for example, because the best way to lose weight is to cut carbs, but they settle my stomach. If I want to eat vegetables (besides cucumber), I have to take a pill in advance. When

I'm traveling, especially, the rules are more important because traveling is unpredictable, but that's precisely when I can get lazy or in denial. I sometimes feel a pang of regret that I can't honor the late, great Anthony Bourdain and eat adventurously; it was particularly sad when I worked at the White House and was traveling around the world to places I'd never dreamed I'd visit. I can dabble with curry and soufflé at home, but I couldn't think of anything more embarrassing than waking up to a headline that read: "DCOS for Ops Shits Self on Official Outing in India!" (I didn't eat much in India, but when I did, I followed the rule anyone who travels a lot will tell you: Only eat local dishes.)

After an entirely self-inflicted incident at an Orange County fund-raiser, I began carrying a change of clothes with me everywhere I went as well; the only thing worse than shitting yourself while traveling for work would be your coworkers having to leave you behind because you shit yourself while traveling for work. At the fund-raiser, they were serving the best food, and I couldn't resist grabbing a piece of quiche. One of my strategies for dealing with anxiety had been to tell everyone who spent any significant amount of time with me about my IBS—because shame = anxiety = more IBS; plus, the more people who know, the more people who can help and support you—so Pfeiffer[2] eyed me with weary dismay.

---

2   As in Dan Pfeiffer, former senior adviser to POTUS, current co-host of *Pod Save America*, *New York Times*–bestselling author of *Yes We (Still) Can: Politics in the Age of Obama, Twitter, and Trump*, and my longtime BFF.

"Don't eat that," he said. "You know what's going to happen."

"I'm just having a little bit of it!" I cried, cutting the smallest portion possible and showing him my fork. It was basically nothing!

After I scarfed my tiniest bite of quiche, basically nothing, we had to make our way back to the vans to hitch Marine One back to LA. As soon as we shut the doors and were on the road I began sweating. A look of terror twitched onto my face. Pfeiffer, having been with me on the entire journey, didn't shift into "I told you so" mode until it was all over. Favs[3] was there, too. They were shouting, "It's OK, Alyssa! You're going to make it!" like I was in the final stretch of a marathon. I'm sure the driver was weirded out because I was indeed breathing like I was finishing a marathon. Or in labor.

I did make it, but not before sweating through my clothes.

But wait, there's more: The time I almost shit my pants in front of the pope because I couldn't resist bad hotel eggs. The time my stomach started to rumble while I was on a boat en route to Gorée in Senegal—probably because it was so hot—and while Pfeiffer was trying to get me to calm down, VJ[4] thought the whole thing was so cute that she took a photo. (I look much happier than I was—she didn't realize I was in the middle of a Poo Terror.) The

---

3   As in Jon Favreau, former speechwriter, current co-host of *Pod Save America*, and another essential member of the crew I (affectionately) refer to as "the bros" in the White House.

4   Valerie Jarrett, former senior adviser to POTUS.

all-time worst moment, though, was when I had gone to dinner in Chicago and decided to walk home when that urgent, panicked feeling washed over me and I broke into a construction site to use a port-o-potty. I used my scarf as toilet paper and, well, the scarf was never seen again.

Now that I no longer work at the White House—and have, crucially, exclusively taken jobs that allow me to show up to work in pajama-esque jumpsuits—I try not to let it affect my life too much. I've learned to be aware of certain things other people might take for granted. Being far from a bathroom stresses me out; you know that moment when you're about to leave a restaurant and are debating whether to use the bathroom because you don't know when you'll be near another one? That's my life all the time. (I prefer taking trains to planes because there are multiple bathrooms on a train; on the Obama campaign in 2007 we started off flying on tiny planes with no bathrooms, or planes with tiny bathrooms equipped with privacy-limiting folding doors, and it made me anxious.) It took me a long time to get where I am, which is acceptance with some self-deprecating humor. Don't be like me: Get to know your body, its strengths and weaknesses, and once you figure out your special-snowflake situation, don't fight it. Figure out specific strategies for making it not suck, and try not to be ashamed. I'm a forty-two-year-old woman with the diet of a picky seven-year-old and the bathroom habits of a seventy-two-year-old. What can I do but talk about it?

SEVEN THINGS IN MY BAG

- Chinese ginger-orange chews and Gas-X: These can calm an angry stomach. The Gas-X makes champagne, salads, and Mexican food much more enjoyable.
- Dental floss: When I got my wisdom teeth removed, the rest of my teeth spaced out; I can basically get an entire roast beef sandwich stuck between my molars.
- Patchouli oil: It's all of who I am. It smells great and is soothing. I walk into the room in a cloud of patchouli and everyone suddenly feels relaxed and gives me exactly what I want.
- Phone charger: My friend Cleo got me one of these weird little iPhone chargers that look like cats and can hold the charge for two phones.
- Eyeglass wipes: I am a pig. My fingerprints are all over everything all the time. These work for glasses and for my iPhone.
- Lip balm and Abreva: I get cold sores, which I find disgusting. I'm never going to reclaim my cold sores and become proud of them. Abreva and lip balm can shut them down quick enough that the virus doesn't colonize my entire mouth.
- Cash: I still live with the fear I experienced as a twenty-three-year-old when my credit card was once declined.

Are You There, God? It's Me, Alyssa

I got my first period flying over the Pacific Ocean. I was in the seventh grade, and we were taking a family trip to Hawaii—very '70s, I know. It was just like when the Brady Bunch went to Hawaii, except there were only two children and no racist cursed tiki dolls. We went to Hawaii because my dad was repelled by the cost of Disney World, and despite being halfway around the globe and home to some of the places that inspired Disney World's Polynesian Village, Hawaii was cheaper.

There was some turbulence. This was back in the days when not every plane was overbooked, and people's definitely-not-regulation carry-ons didn't spring forth from the overhead compartments like Olympic sprinters any time you hit rough air, so there was an empty seat between me and my sister. I was scared during the turbulence, so I thought I wet myself. The Fasten Seat Belt signs were still on, so I had to sit (literally) with this assumption for a few minutes. Not only were we going to crash into a fiery/watery grave only to then be eaten by a shark, but my last seconds would be spent wearing urine-soaked underwear. Terrible. What if my family took a moment out of their screaming and praying to notice? When we could finally get out of our seats again, I went to the bathroom and saw the telltale splotch. A teeny bit of blood. I freaked out.

I didn't freak out because I thought I was dying. I knew what periods were, and I knew mine was coming. I had just dreaded it, ever since, as an advanced reader in the second grade, I'd learned from an outdated edition of *Are You There God? It's Me, Margaret* that you had to wear gigantic diaper-esque maxi pads that came with belts. Belts! There was no mention of tampons. As a curious premenarche preteen I'd taken a few moseys down the feminine hygiene aisle and felt so confused. There were no belts anywhere!

I eventually figured out that technology had advanced beyond diaper belts—my friend Kim's older sister showed us tampons when I was eight or nine, though I still didn't understand what they did. That didn't stop me from crying at her demonstration—I couldn't believe I would have to endure whatever it was they were. And beyond the practical concerns, there was the mythology. For people who get periods, telling the story of the moment you got your first is almost as much a rite of passage as actually getting it, so I'd been building it up. Would it bleed through my pants without my noticing? Would it happen at school? In bed? What would I be wearing? My sister was useless—she's four years younger than I am! I was jealous of her because she had so much period-free time ahead of her. Someday my life as a non-period-having person would end, and I would be a period-haver! I didn't know the specifics of what having a period entailed, but I knew it was *bad*.

In retrospect this is consistent with how I react to any change: I resist it dramatically. Every year that passed when I didn't have to learn how to use a tampon felt like I was dodging the draft.

And then Aunt Flo arrived. I thought it was disgusting. I didn't tell my mom because I was hoping it would go away, so instead I took toilet paper from the airplane lavatory and rolled it around my underwear. (No one taught me this—I think it's instinctual knowledge all women carry with them from birth.)

So the rest of the plane ride was fine. But how was I going to get through a beach vacay without letting it slip that I needed a tampon but had no idea how to use one?

Well, I'd read a lot about periods by that point. I knew that periods can be irregular at first, so I hoped it wouldn't last long and I could just wing it. I was also under the impression that your period stops when you're in water, which was convenient.[1] I could do the TP roll when we

---

1 When I told co-author Lauren that this was a common line about periods, she didn't believe me. I don't envy millennials very often, but I do think they got the better end of the deal when it comes to sex ed. Mostly. There are still abstinence-only schools—bad—but things have come a long way. When I was in eighth grade we took a multiple-choice test in health class that included the following question:
    Which of these ways can you contract AIDS?
    a) sitting on a toilet seat
    b) kissing
    c) holding hands
    d) all of the above
    I can't remember what I thought the answer was, but my best friend,

were drinking virgin daiquiris next to the pig roast and then nip away to the loo to remove it before going down to the beach. They also tell you that if you go into the water with your period you'll make yourself vulnerable to attack from sharks, which can allegedly smell the blood, but the incompatibility between these two pieces of wisdom did nothing to make me question either. I went into the water thinking I wouldn't bleed through my suit while also keeping an eye out for Jaws.

Nothing disastrous happened either way, but I still feel I was right to dread the decades of menstruation ahead of me. I have my fair share of *bled through my white pants* stories. (The worst was during the tenth-grade band trip, and I bled all the way through my pants and onto the seat and spent most of the journey embarrassed and trying to scrub it out.) I also had terrible cramps. I know many women think we should be celebrating our periods and the miracle of life they represent, and I get it—they're still considered shameful in much of the world, and even in America. I'm not advocating for shame. Tampons should be free! Everyone

---

Cara, knew the question wasn't right, so she didn't answer it. Then she got into an argument with the teacher about it, who claimed that the correct answer was "all of the above." Stupid. (To be totally clear, the answer is none of the above.)

Anyway, to resolve this dispute between me and Lauren about whether getting your period in water is a thing, we googled "Do you get your period in water?" and the first result was an article called "10 Period Myths You Shouldn't Believe" on Seventeen.com. So I guess we were both right: It was a thing, just a wrong thing. And according to the article, your period doesn't stop in water, but it can slow down and may not flow because of counterpressure.

should talk about their periods! Growing up I felt as though I had to suffer in silence, and as a result I didn't think there was anything I could do about the attendant miseries of my monthly cycle, so I ended up in pain and publicly bleeding through my pants. (If you read my first book, you may remember that I didn't stop bleeding through my pants as an adult employee of the Obama White House—sure. But that was because of laziness and a lack of preparation, not shame.)[2]

Still, I don't think that the project of destigmatizing periods is incompatible with acknowledging that they aren't fun and that life would be a lot better if we didn't have them. The point is that periods both suck and are an unavoidable part of life. There's no reason we should make them suck worse by refusing to discuss them. From my perspective, in the midst of perimenopause, it's fucking annoying that I had to go through it at all. My actual period has reverted to being as hellish as it was in high school, and I'm still on the NuvaRing because it kept me from having really bad periods when I was younger and now I'm terrified to even imagine how bad they'd be if I stopped. Everything that you dealt with in high school that you thought was over in your twenties and thirties comes back with a vengeance in your forties, except that in your forties you get the bonus of also being really hot all the time. And I don't mean hot as in sexy. I had to get one of those fans you plug into your

---

2   I'll repeat the advice I gave in my first book, which is to never leave the house without at least two tampons and a Tide stick.

iPhone! All this uterine drama feels like it's for nothing, too, because I can't even have kids! Some women think that if you don't have a baby, menopause is *worse*? Who came up with that? Is the point to try to make it even? Like, OK, you guys had to be pregnant for nine months and undergo LABOR, so the women who don't have kids should have to endure at least *some* kind of additional reproduction-related suffering. It's only fair!

SEVEN THINGS IN MY MEDICINE CABINET

- Kate Somerville ExfoliKate and EradiKate are two of the best products I have ever used. They aren't cheap, but they last a long time. The young among you will be happy to know that the deliciously painful period zits you look forward to every month return with a vengeance in your forties (or at least they have for me). As long as I DON'T PICK THEM, this stuff works.
- Safety pins: V-necks don't fit me quite right—too much cleave—so I am crafty with the pins. Good thing to carry in your purse as well for surprise wardrobe malfunctions (yours or a friend's).
- Ponds Cream for Dry Skin: I have savagely dry elbows!
- Goody headband: If you follow me on Instagram, this will occasionally make an appearance—I have bangs and need something to get them out of my face while I do all the stuff I need to do to prevent zits. I also have a shower cap to spare my blowouts.
- CBD pills and drops: I too am on the CBD train. It helps you relax!
- L'Oréal Age Perfect Cell Renewal Rosy Tone Moisturizer: Gives you a very nice "alive" look even when you feel dead. The downside is that when I wash my face at night,

there is some pink on the face towel, which irritates me. I could get a pink face towel, I guess.

- Dosist vape pens: They vibrate when you've gotten exactly 2.25 mg (one dose)! I recommend them to everyone I know! Weed should be legal!

When John Kerry Saw Me in My Underwear

John Kerry's 2004 "Sea to Shining Sea" tour ran from Boston, Massachusetts, to Portland, Oregon, and it had almost as many slogans—it was also called "Believe in America," and about ten other things—as it did complicated logistical maneuvers. To travel nearly three thousand miles through twenty-two states in fifteen days, we took buses to a ferry to more buses to a train to more buses; helicopters and planes were also involved. We were traveling with the entire Kerry family and the entire Edwards family, and by the time we got to Kansas City—can't remember if it was Missouri or Kansas—we had to pause the trip, take an unplanned daylong break so they could all rest, and push everything back a full day, which created a domino effect of disasters and scheduling conflicts that involved, ultimately, more traveling, because the city we'd planned to stay in one night had no vacancies in any hotel because it was hosting a regional Little League World Series tournament. My gums were bleeding by the end, and we were delirious from exhaustion.

The last leg of the last bus portion went through Death Valley, spitting us out in Santa Monica for a dinner and beach party for the press before we would finish things off in Oregon. (We had to end on the latter "shining sea"— get it? I maintain that our absurd conceptual confusion is why we lost.) Everyone was looking forward to this dinner, which would signify not only that we were nearing the end of this self-imposed odyssey but also that we were in California, which is really nice.

There comes a point during a campaign when you stop thinking about anything but the immediate task in front of you. For me, this point had come and gone days or weeks before we all arrived at our hotel in Santa Monica, when we had a blissful hour or so to get ready before the party. As soon as I got to the room I was sharing with Doug, my boyfriend, the immediate task in front of me became: shower. It was really hot in the room, too, so showering would have the added benefit of making me less sweaty.

When you travel with Secret Service, your bags need to be inspected, and then they're brought to your room, so you always leave the hotel door open so someone can drop them off. I did this without a thought and went on with my shower plan.

While I was in the shower, someone must have brought our bags in, because when I got out there was a ton of stuff in our hallway, including JK's Tour de France–style bike. JK's overachieving spirit was evident in the scope and ambition of this tour, so when I tell you that he also brought his fancy bike everywhere, it should make sense. I was so dazed that I didn't notice it or register its significance in our room—part of Doug's job was to handle all JK's stuff.

I had managed to put on a T-shirt and a pair of pink underwear when I got the idea to turn on the radio. "Dancing on the Ceiling" filled the room. In that moment, nothing could have been better. I was clean. I was groovy. I turned it up and decided to take a break from getting dressed to lie on the bed. It was like I hadn't lain on a bed in months, maybe years! I spread my arms wide to take up space and began to sort of shimmy my shoulders as I lay on my back. I was so excited to be lying down that I began to space out a bit. I was the star of a movie about a spunky independent girl who's just moved to New York and gotten her dream job and is now celebrating by lying in bed and dancing to Lionel Richie. Or maybe I was proto–Hannah Horvath in *Girls*. This reverie lasted about thirty seconds, until I heard the door open and saw presidential candidate Senator John Kerry materialize in front of me, saying something about his bike.

Neither of us said a word, and my instincts kicked in. I grabbed the edge of the comforter and rolled myself up like a burrito. He took his bike, and from my hiding place I heard it click out of the room.

The practical advice here is to always lock your doors—it won't kill the Secret Service to have to knock!

The spiritual advice is a little more satisfying. Today I'd characterize myself as someone who gives no fucks, who understands that accidents happen and who can laugh about them relatively soon after. But at the risk of sounding trite, the world was very different back then! We had no Lena Dunham dancing in her underwear on HBO. We had no mainstream body-positivity movement. I was definitely thinner than I am now, but I didn't feel thin. Even ignoring the fact that it was my boss and that my boss was John Kerry, I was so ashamed to be seen without my clothes on— seen doing something *super dorky* without my clothes on— that I didn't go to the party that night.

I do wish I'd gone. Self-consciousness about your body— even if it comes from the totally legitimate mortification of your important boss seeing you in your underwear— shouldn't prevent you from living your life. If I'd been there, JK and I might have shared a knowing, mutually embarrassed look and then laughed it off. As it is, I'll never know how much he saw, and I don't want to.

The Meow Coat Has Claws

I don't think I ever looked good before the age of twenty-six. My taste was way off, and there was way too much not wearing a bra for the size and shape of my boobs. Because I am 5 feet 2 inches and dumpling-shaped, I was not ideally suited to trends set almost exclusively by Kate Moss and the Spice Girls, but I always wanted to fit in with everyone else. In high school, that meant I wore a lot of bodysuits. My favorite was from the Gap—three-quarter-sleeved; striped in red, navy, white, and green; and scoop neck—and I wore it with my dad's navy sweatpants, with the waistband rolled down.[1]

In college and after, everyone was wearing bebe spaghetti-strap tank tops, and since I was taught that showing a bra strap made you look "trashy," the obvious solution was to

---

[1] I was going to say that it seems weird that everyone loved to wear sweatpants in high school, but then I remembered that everyone wears sweatpants (or leggings) now, too. The roll, though—you don't really see that in places that don't have lockers.

skip the bra altogether. I never tried things on in the store because the lighting always seemed like a personal attack on me and I assumed I could just, in the words of Tim Gunn, "make it work" once I got home. This does not make any sense at all. Using this philosophy, I once bought pleather pants from Century 21 in order to look like a little sexy kitten at the bar, and although I was able to get them on at the beginning of my night out, by the time I got home, I'd swelled up because it was warm outside, so I couldn't get them off. My roommate had to cut me out of them. Just like Olivia Newton-John on the set of *Grease*, except I couldn't sing or dance and I had impressed zero Danny Zukos while out on the town. At least they weren't expensive. In the professional arena, I would don my faux cashmere periwinkle turtleneck that I was convinced made my boobs look good, regardless of the effect it had on my savage sweating problem. I usually paired it with a black Banana Republic skirt that never fit right.

In other words, my early twenties were a time-lapse BEFORE photo that I prepared for by overenthusiastically putting on clothes and being like, *LOOK! Clothes!* I also always cut my hair on a whim, if I was feeling depressed or bored, and I often fell into the trap of thinking that, by bringing my hairstylist a photo of a gorgeous celebrity, I would leave the salon looking like the person with the haircut. (Usually Mandy Moore.) It didn't help that all my haircuts were done by vagabonds who wouldn't try to reason with you or gently pose the possibility that perhaps your face shape isn't quite right for "side-swept bangs." In college I dyed my hair black in an effort to become Janeane Garofalo in *Reality Bites*. I also wore a lot of scrunchies, which I collected. Hillary Clinton walking off the plane in Vietnam in a giant scrunchie was personally vindicating for me.

Now I know what works on my body and only shop from brands whose sizing I understand, and I also organize my life so that I never have to wear anything one might call "business casual." Besides a very brief stint with lavender dye at the beginning of my job at Vice—I wanted to let loose!—my hairdresser tells it to me like it is. Although my friend Stacy London (of *What Not to Wear*) will occasionally comment on one of my selfies with a skeptical emoji—I like to mix patterns!—I know she means it in a loving way.

I know she does.

She definitely does.

But developing this confidence took a long time. It wasn't that I was unaware that I was dressing inappropriately, exactly. Something always felt off. I would look in the mirror and see that the clothes didn't look good, but I thought that was my fault, not the clothes'. I think even stereotypically beautiful and thin women feel this way, but I do have photographic evidence (which I refuse to look at) that I looked especially like someone who took her signature look in equal parts from her big sister's and dad's closets. Almost all my fashion choices were guided by my desire to look cute up top and cover my booty, but I don't have the greatest boobs, so this plan was flawed from the get-go. I was trying to dress myself into a body I was never going to have.

My worst outfit ever was my New Year's Eve 1999 ensemble. I'd saved my overtime check to buy a Betsey Johnson jacket I'd seen at Century 21 called the Meow Coat: a black, crushed-velvet, single-button number with Cookie Monster–looking fur cuffs and lining. I decided that this was to be the centerpiece of my NYE look, so the rest of the outfit was my idea of understated: a bebe tank top (sans bra), a summery black viscose skirt, last-minute Wolford black tights that I had to spend forty dollars on because the ones I had ripped, and black Steve Madden platform Mary Janes that one of my roommates, Amy Volpe, made me keep under the bed because they smelled so bad. Artificial materials retain odors.

The gang was going to Sequoia on the waterfront, a very Wall Street place that had a $125 cover for drinks and meat on a stick. (I couldn't identify what type of meat—it was a loose interpretation of satay, which was trendy at the time.) It was over my budget, but it was also New Year's, and my coat needed an occasion worthy of its various fabrics. It was the most adventurous thing I'd ever worn, and in the apartment before we set out I couldn't stop admiring how "glam" I looked in it.

As soon as we got to Sequoia, the door girls told me I'd have to take it off. And pay ten dollars to check it.

I had not considered this at all. The prospect of abandoning the Meow Coat to the depths of the overpriced coat check was unthinkable. I began to bargain.

I first made an appeal to personal liberty. Why should I have to pay an additional ten dollars when I would be happy to keep my coat on in the club? I didn't want to hand over my pride and joy to the bored coat-check girls; I preferred to keep it on my person at all times.

The door girls were unyielding.

I tried a more ontological approach. "It's not a coat," I said, gesturing to its impractical single button and demonstrating its relative thinness to the implacable doorman. "It's my *outfit*."

Investing too much emotional energy in your clothes will only lead to disappointment and inflexibility. My friends were all standing in the doorway beyond, looking sad for me but also, *Just check your coat like everyone else so we can get our gin and tonics*, they were saying with their eyes. The door girls shook their heads. Removing the Meow Coat and revealing the boring top and bottom beneath felt like a defeat. When no one talked to me—but couldn't stop chatting up the rest of my friends—I was convinced it was because my outfit sucked. I left at 11:30 before the fireworks and ate a slice of pizza on the walk from the South Street Seaport back to SoHo. On top of everything else, the coat wasn't warm enough.

SEVEN THINGS IN MY CLOSET

- Grateful Dead wool sweaters from Granted sweater company in British Columbia. I hope they live forever. And even if they don't, I'll probably still keep them.
- Lots of jeans that don't fit and never will again, but because they were expensive and fit once, I hold on to them.
- Woolrich plaid overalls.
- A few memorable shirts, including my Kate Spades, that I would wear regularly at the White House. All my other White House clothes went to Dress for Success years ago.
- Matching sweats from the Great, which I wear like real clothes out in the real world.
- More clogs and Birkenstocks than are probably reasonable.
- Warning: eye-watering price tag ahead— my Valentino Couture hand-embroidered wedding dress that I guiltily and stressfully paid $13,550 for (on a serious payment plan...) and ended up not wearing to my wedding (or anywhere else) because it seemed too fancy. I know this is going to make me seem extremely fancy. I promise I will wear it someday.

What to Expect When You're Not Expecting to Ride a Motorcycle Hundreds of Miles Along the Japanese Coast

I didn't sign up for Introduction to Japanese during my freshman year of college for any good reason, which is sometimes the best reason. It was neither a bad idea nor a good idea—it was just an idea, inspired, as both bad and good ideas often are, by the sighting of a hot guy.

When I was in college, we registered for classes the old-fashioned way: by physically lining up behind a table in the gym so you could write your name down on a list. Priorities were critical; you might forfeit every other choice by wasting the precious first minutes of sign-ups to pause and think about whether you'd prefer Lesbian Vampires in Film and Literature or the History of Beer. However, because I like to see where life takes me, I planned only my core classes, and by the time I registered for all of them I had one wildcard spot left open. I was wondering what to do when I looked over and saw him.

There's no other word for how he looked but groovy. He was about 6 feet 4 inches, with wild, curly blond hair, and despite being really hot, he exuded friendliness. (Hot people are usually intimidating, right?) And he was standing in the line for Japanese 101. I sidled up behind him. Maybe it would be fun.

His name was David Fogel, and the bonds of sharing introductory language course humiliations meant we became fast friends (though I remained, spoiler alert, in the friend zone—the same humiliations that create lasting platonic connections probably also snuff out romantic sparks). We stayed in touch after I transferred from the University of Vermont to Wisconsin, and when he graduated and moved to Hokkaido, in northern Japan, to teach English, he told me I should come visit.

I had spent a lot of time and energy to learn pretty decent Japanese, and I felt like I needed to go.[1] I saved my

---

1   Years later, the White House planned a trip to Asia that swung through Japan. Though I was rusty on the language, I began brushing up beforehand so I could impress everyone—particularly the younger employees, many of whom were from the Midwest—with my skills. The night we arrived, I decided to take everyone out for sushi and show off. My display began at the concierge, whom I asked for a recommendation in what I thought was good, if not perfect, Japanese. We'd flown overnight and were super tired— I wasn't worried about messing up, which usually helps you not mess up.

We were all having a great time at the restaurant, ordering rounds of yakis and toris. Then, about halfway through the meal—I don't know how I missed it before—I realized that, despite my competent Japanese, which I'd believed signaled me as a nuanced traveler and not some basic tourist, the concierge had sent us to Nobu. Wind, meet sails.

The next morning, I got a knock on my door at around 6:00 AM. "Boss," Reggie Love, Obama's body man, said. "Boss wants to see you."

paralegal overtime, combined with all the American Airlines miles I racked up flying back and forth between Madison and New York during my last two years of college, and went. Booking plane tickets is so easy now—if not exactly fun—but twenty years ago you did it on the phone, with no twenty-four-hour window to change your mind. Because this was so much money to me—all my money, in fact— I made my dad help. Unlike the time when I was around fourteen and my parents made me use my newly acquired French to book the hotel for our family vacation to Paris— setting my destiny to become a scheduling and advance person—he agreed.

David and I had been emailing in preparation, and he'd told me to dress warm. Since it was April, I assumed that meant bring a jean jacket and a sweatshirt. Famous last words. There was no way for me to look up the weather in Hokkaido at the time, and I'd skipped buying a guidebook— the pickings back then were slim. But to be fair I'd also not counted on David picking me up on his motorcycle.

POTUS couldn't sleep and wanted to convene a meeting of senior staff; in my sweats, I followed David Axelrod, fully decked out in Chicago sports paraphernalia pj's, down the hallway.

As we were all drinking coffee in POTUS's suite, I inserted a non sequitur. I know no one likes dream stories, but the one I'd just had was particularly vivid, and I felt I needed to tell someone about it. We were all friends, and I had shared much dumber dream stories than this one. "Guys, I had this dream where I fell off a cliff," I said. "It really felt like I was falling, too!"

I saw the people around the room make polite *Oh, that's interesting* faces to indicate they were not interested. But then Robert Gibbs chimed in. "Huh. I had a dream where I fell off something, too."

Finally, Secret Service explained that there had been a 4.7 earthquake in the middle of the night. We'd all been so tired that we slept through it.

◆ ◆ ◆

Why did I not count on David picking me up on his motorcycle? I don't know. I knew he was buying one, but because both motorcycles and Japan were abstract concepts to me at the time, I guess I couldn't imagine being *on* a motorcycle *in* Japan. Since I had moved to New York, I thought I was really cool, so I arrived with my jean jacket and impractically gigantic Kenneth Cole weekend bag (purchased at Marshall's). As soon as I saw David, who met me at Narita, his face fell. "Oh…," he said, in a disappointed tone that sounded like I had just given him socks for his birthday. "You're gonna be cold."

I contemplated this on the train we took to where the motorcycle was parked.

Like childbirth—I have to assume—the romance of riding a motorcycle obscures the realities of experiencing it. The helmet is sweaty and tight on your head, and once you get going, the whole thing shakes you the entire time. It hurts, and the effort required to hang on is a lot—particularly if you have very short legs. I knew I was going to be sore.

We'd been driving for about half an hour before the lights flashed behind us. There was a siren, but it was like a baby siren. It's always interesting to hear emergency sirens in foreign countries—Japanese sirens sound very non-menacing. We pulled over, and I started to panic. We hadn't been speeding, so I had no idea what it could be about. Had I committed some grave error at customs and been tailed by authorities the entire time? Was David on the run? Involved in some elaborate cheese-smuggling ring? (Something as wholesome as cheese is the only thing I can imagine him smuggling.) Regardless, my vacation was off to a great start.

Within Tokyo—but not in the rest of Japan—it's illegal to have two people riding on a motorcycle. This was how it was in 1999, at least. We explained the situation—well, mainly David; I didn't have my Japanese confidence yet—and the police drove me to the city limits. They were very friendly, and there was no barricade in the car, so I soon found myself sitting in the back seat of a Toyota Corolla practicing my vocabulary on the Tokyo police. We discussed the weather, what brought me to Japan, and what it was like to live in New York. Language practice in a jail cell might have been more comprehensive, but I have to say I'm glad I never got *that* opportunity.

After they pulled over and let me out, we drove a couple of more hours to the home of the host family David stayed with during college. Two aspects of this visit were nerve-racking: (1) The reason David's Japanese was so good was that none of them spoke English, and (2) men and women traveling together without being married was not so much of a thing at the time. Luckily I had any anxiety shaken out of me—literally—as we progressed up the family's rocky driveway. The bike stalled, and the sudden jolt of the stop combined with the way I'd wrangled my awkward, heavy bag onto my back sent me flying backward, rolling down the hill with my Kenneth Cole.

You know how they say that babies often leave car

accidents uninjured because they're so relaxed and don't know what's going on? I was so loopy from the flight and the hours of clinging to David on his roaring motorcycle that I just bounced—definitely at least one concrete bounce.

"Are you OK?!?!" David yelled down after me.

"Hai...," I replied (Japanese for "yes"), and trudged back up the hill. Although the family was nice, my jet lag combined with my recent tumble meant I didn't have it in me to respond to their totally comprehensible Japanese. Instead of trying to get through it politely I said I was tired and went to sleep.

◆　◆　◆

Back on the road the next day, things were glorious. I'd slept some time-warping number of hours on a bed that was not a mat on the floor. Our itinerary was to drive up along the west coast of Honshu, the biggest island, stay the night on the way, and then hop a ferry the next night to Hokkaido. That night, we'd get to see a beautiful sunset over the Sea of Japan. It was cold, yes, but not that cold.

But first: I realized I was getting my period.

I poked David in the ribs—maybe a little too forcefully considering he was in charge of my life—and screamed into his ear: "WHEN WE STOP TO GET GAS I NEED TO USE THE BATHROOM!" He said: "WHAT?" And I said: "BATHROOM!!!!" And he nodded.

The thing about tampons in Japan is that they were not prevalent at the time, particularly in the more rural towns we were traveling through. As my readers will know well, now I overstock my bag with several variations of feminine hygiene products, but at age twenty-three I was still a fly-by-the-seat-of-my-(stained)-pants kind of girl. I assumed I'd be able to get them. Not so. Although I was disappointed in the lack of urgency in his warnings about the weather (or maybe just my lack of attention to that detail), David had no way to know that the tampon availability situation would be dire. Besides, this was still back in the days when women didn't necessarily discuss their bodily functions, and men certainly didn't. Me and the four or five spare tampons I had rolling around at the bottom of my bag were on our own.

The gas station, like many public places in Japan, was equipped with a squat toilet, aka a hole in the ground. My legs were so tired that I worried I would collapse and fall in. As I was hovering painfully over the hole, I looked down and noticed the entirety of both inner thighs was bruised, from knee to cooch. There should be more *What to Expect When You're Not Expecting to Ride a Motorcycle for Hundreds of Miles but Somehow You Ended Up on One* books. Or at least blog posts!

Because I wanted to prove to David that I was a go-with-the-flow kind of girl, breezily beautiful wearing just a swipe of mascara and a ponytail—I am not this person—I did not make my problem known. If I had, he probably could have helped me. Or taken me somewhere that sold pads. Instead, I reckoned I'd have to ration the tampons because we were getting more remote, not less.

Another thing I learned about riding motorcycles is that you have a lot of time alone, thinking your thoughts. Mine were mainly about my aching thighs, being cold (and getting colder), and whether I was going to bleed all over my gracious host's Yamaha. One of my favorite things about driving is listening to music, so to distract myself from my multifaceted physiological predicament I decided to see how much of Bruce Springsteen's discography I could sing by heart. I figured David couldn't hear me, because I couldn't hear me.

When we finally reached our home for the night, a hostel with tatami mats on the floor, I rejoiced to see there was a real bathroom. I figured that every time I found one, I could use the handy toilet-paper roll-around to conserve my supply. I would also stuff extra in the Kenneth Cole.

The next day we set off for the ferry to get us to Hokkaido, and that was when I felt a real shift in the weather. I'd thought I was cold before, but now I was really fucking cold. My jean jacket was cute but not cutting it. David, who was fully decked out in a winter coat, gloves, and a hat, offered me one of these items of clothing approximately every ten minutes.

"No, no, don't worry!" I said cheerfully, my cheeks frozen in a fake smile/grimace. "I'm fine!"

I wasn't fine by any stretch. I was happy to spend the night on the ferry.

◆　◆　◆

It was lightly snowing as we disembarked the ferry the next morning. He saw the look of wincing panic on my face. "We're just gonna go as fast as we can," he assured me. "No stops."

The effort of lugging around the Kenneth Cole didn't produce enough warmth. Not even *Born to Run* could distract me from the way my fingers seemed to be detaching from my body. After about an hour I punched him in the back. "CAN I HAVE YOUR GLOVES?" I screamed.

Even so, when we finally arrived in the small town where David taught, I was freezing. His house was cold and damp because he'd been gone for a while, and didn't have a ton of hot water. When I informed him of my plan to warm myself up in the bath, I was thwarted by how shallow it was: The water came up to mid-shin when I was sitting down. Very *Little House on the Prairie*, but without the cool outfits. *Iron Chef* hadn't yet premiered in America, and it was the perfect level of Japanese to make just enough sense while I was falling asleep. (Remaining tampon count: two. Ruined underwear count: two.)

The next night, we got invited to a dinner with some of the older men in town. If this seems weird, let me explain: Everyone in this town was in awe of David. Picture a tall, curly-headed, blond, friendly American who spoke near-perfect Japanese descending on a small town of a few hundred people. Women of all ages would giggle when he walked by. On our way to the restaurant, David told me that they didn't usually invite women to eat at the table at these dinners, but "they're making a special exception for you."

Now, I haven't mentioned food yet in this essay. If you didn't skip the IBS essay in this book out of disgust, you will find this odd. But I wasn't eating enough for it to matter. The food thus far in the trip had been pretty bland and unremarkable—road food, gyoza, rice, that kind of thing. But this dinner is where the real Japanese food, the unheard-of stuff, came into play.

I was aware that the men had made a special exception for me, so I would have to eat whatever was put in front of me to be polite. The first courses were delicious. But then came the uni, or urchin, which I'd never had before and still believe is best described as snot. When it was set down in front of me, I knew I had to eat it, so I put it in my mouth. But as soon as I put it in my mouth, I knew that eating it would be impossible. Most people would think to raise their napkin daintily and discreetly to their mouths, deposit the offending foodstuff into it, and move on with the meal. I, however, felt everyone would surely suspect what I was doing if I put my napkin up to my mouth. So I waited until everyone was talking and spit the uni into my lap, only marginally more polite than Tom Hanks tasting caviar in *Big*.[2] It slithered into the cuff of my pants, at which point I panicked and tried to brush it onto the floor. When I got home to New York I found I'd lost more than ten pounds.

---

2 A major international incident occurred in 1992, when, at a state dinner in Japan weeks before the New Hampshire primary, President George H. W. Bush vomited in the lap of Prime Minister Kiichi Miyazawa and then passed out. The term *"Bushu-suru"* was subsequently coined, to mean "to do the Bush thing."

The rest of the trip passed smoothly and uneventfully and was honestly a lot of fun, though it was a great example of how not being prepared can fucking suck. It was a once-in-a-lifetime experience that would have been so much better with some long underwear and a bounty of tampons.

David had to teach on my last day—he'd picked me up because it was a holiday, but when it was time to go back to Tokyo for my return flight, I had to do it on my own. The night before I had to leave he explained how to get there: Take a bus to a town where I would wait on a street corner for another bus. This bus would transport me to a small airport, where I would take a flight to the other, non-Narita airport (Haneda) in Tokyo, from which I would take a train to Narita for my flight. I was nervous, but I also felt like if I could make it on a motorcycle trip with four tampons and no gloves, I could do pretty much anything.

As he was leaving me to go to sleep, he looked back. "I love *Born to Run*, too," he said. When I expressed shock that he could have possibly heard me at all, he replied that he could hear me the entire time.

Oh, the Places You'll Go! (And Be Spied on by Foreign Governments)

For a while, there was a joke going around social media that Donald Trump was afraid of stairs. (The word for this fear, FYI, is "bathmophobia.") In the weeks after he was inaugurated, photos and videos surfaced of him conspicuously avoiding inclines and steps. He grabbed Theresa May's hand as the pair walked down a ramp at the White House, beaming the entire time like a baby who's just discovered his reflection, as if that were not really weird. An anonymous source in a *Washington Post* article said he wouldn't go to Kellyanne Conway's office because it was on the second floor. Jezebel reasoned that his fear of stairs was proven by the fact that he can often be seen gripping handrails on his way up and down despite his public fear of germs. A CNN reporter even talked about it on *New Day*. While I do not want to associate myself with Trump through any other quality, I have to admit I don't begrudge him this particular alleged phobia. I hate going down stairs, too.

I have vertigo—yes, in addition to IBS; kind of a mess

over here—which means I've almost fallen down the stairs in many countries. It's better now, but when I worked in the White House it was particularly bad. Traveling with the president meant I was often in countries with no obligation to be ADA-compliant, staring down a flight of stairs that I was not confident I could conquer without concussing myself and showing dignitaries my Hanes Her Way. I usually coped by clinging to the railings like a woman who got her hands on the last 60 percent off Vera Wang dress at the annual Kleinfeld's Bridal sale and was not letting go despite it being two sizes too small.

The first time I ever noticed my vertigo was when I was working for John Kerry and he was interviewing vice presidential candidates. In order to maintain some dignity in the process and not let the names leak, we went to great pains to keep the interviewees sequestered away. Kerry was meeting with Bill Richardson—then the governor of New Mexico, before that the secretary of energy and the ambassador to the UN—in Phoenix. The interview was a few flights from the ground floor, and Richardson asked me for coffee in a cup with a saucer. (Why? Who knows.) The kitchen was on a higher floor, so I went to get it. But once I had the coffee (with the saucer), I had to walk down about three flights of stairs. I remember thinking that this was how I was going to die—or at the very least trip, fall forward, and knock out my front teeth. I was ultimately glad Richardson had requested that saucer—it was a lot easier not to spill hot coffee on myself while I was slowly creeping down the stairs.

After that I tried to only wear flats, which helps a bit. But sometimes the situation was more complicated. The staircase at the Kremlin is, like, thirty feet wide, with a red carpet down the middle, and there was no way I could politely walk down the side of it without looking like a little kid playing the "Don't step in the lava!" game. Traveling with President Obama, I was always hyperaware of my position as a representative of the US government, and I felt like everyone was watching my every move, waiting for me to slip up so they had an excuse to blame the United States for something. (Often, they actually were, but I'll get to that in a second.) At the Kremlin, trembling at the top of the steps as the rest of the delegation proceeded down like debutantes, I had to get Ben Rhodes to come back and hold my hand so that I wouldn't have to live on the second floor of the Kremlin forever. This also happened at the Great Wall (a nightmare of stairs) and the Colosseum. I didn't go up into the pyramids because I knew I wouldn't be able to get back down. (They have small pyramids, too, which I did visit. The smaller ones are for the ladies, obviously.)

◆ ◆ ◆

It's funny to recall all my travel bloopers now, but unfortunately I have to impart some serious and relevant lessons to you about them. Because at the time they didn't feel funny; they felt like life-or-death situations. It's impossible to avoid messing up while traveling and impossible to avoid it at work, but when the two converge, the stakes multiply.

Especially when you work for the president of the United States. ("Especially when you work for the president of the United States" could be my tagline.) On official trips, what might normally have been a mildly embarrassing faux pas, good fodder for dinner party (or book) anecdotes, becomes a misstep that could cause a diplomatic dispute (and cost you your job). There can be severe consequences if you're insensitive or offensive. Which is the current president's natural state. We haven't seen all the repercussions his (presumably) unplanned diplomacy will have, but it's clear from the stern look plastered on Angela Merkel's face that he's undoing so much of the work Obama put in.

Obama traveled the most of any president during a first year in office—ten trips, twenty-one countries. Why did we do this? Because it's what you do. This is going to sound really obvious, but the Trump presidency has shown that nothing obvious should be taken for granted. It matters which countries you visit and in what order: It's a show of respect and an acknowledgment of your allies' position. Contrast that with Trump, who took four trips to sixteen countries in his first year, and still, as of this writing, hasn't been to Mexico as the president. (His trip as a candidate was deemed a "colossal failure" for Mexicans, according to a Politico article.) There's also the responsibility present in any foreign travel, the hyperawareness that you're in another country and have to be respectful of their culture as you'd hope they'd be respectful of yours, which for some reason I don't think Trump is aware of.

You also have to be prepared for and plan for anything,

which I can't imagine the Trump administration are or does. That Trump tweets from around the world using an unsecured iPhone is another one of those things I have to mention and denounce even though it's painfully obvious that any time you travel anywhere as an employee of the US government people are watching everything you do, and not necessarily with the safety of you and your country in mind.

The first time I was forced to understand this was on our 2009 trip to Saudi Arabia, which, despite my frantic preparation, I nearly flubbed in a few different ways.

Saudi Arabia was the first trip we were really nervous about—there were so many rules and expectations, particularly for women. Though the only very senior gals on this trip were me and Valerie Jarrett, we received a special packing memo: We had to bring light-colored clothes that totally covered ourselves, and we couldn't wear open-toed shoes. We would be staying at King Abdullah's farm (the King Abdullah before this one), but women were not to shake his hand.

As soon as we landed, I had two realizations. The first was that the Saudis had spray-painted all the grass at the farm green. The second was that I'd packed the wrong shoes—the only ones I had demonstrated my piggies very visibly going to market.

I panicked and began shouting. Literally shouting, to everyone in the receiving line, a group that included Denis McDonough and David Axelrod, that I had brought the wrong shoes. It was not the first or last time I'd think, *At least I'm wearing pants.* The boys did not understand.

Because we were senior officials, VJ and I had to go through the greeting line. I was scrunching my toes in a futile attempt to hide them as POTUS introduced us to King Abdullah. Who immediately stuck out his hand toward me. I was like Cindy Brady when she goes on TV and can only stare in wide-eyed horror at the red light that signals the cameras are rolling. I had no idea what to do. Eventually I shook his hand and scooted off.

I wish I hadn't panicked in that moment, because I would like to be able to remember if he had soft hands. I think so. As soon as it was more appropriate, I scampered off and began yapping like a Yorkie at Denis McDonough about whether I'd caused irreparable diplomatic damage and was going to get kicked out of the country. Nobody cared about the shoes, which I also forgot about completely.

From there we all went to lunch, where no one would speak to VJ or me, and then to our assigned villas. Within a few minutes, I got an email from VJ saying her villa was full of jewelry. What was she going to do?

I immediately became enraged. *Nobody gave* me *any jewels!* I thought with a scowl. *Why doesn't anyone take me seriously?!* I emailed her back: I wouldn't know. I didn't get jewels. I hated feeling like I was getting less than other people because I was a "kid."

I was still fuming when she replied to ask if I'd opened the briefcase sitting on the dresser. I had not, but of course it contained a giant ruby-and-diamond necklace, watch, cocktail ring, and bracelet. I put it all on, obviously. I looked like a toddler who broke into a wealthy dowager's jewelry box.

I ran over to VJ's (sans jewelry—I wasn't about to lose a ruby), and we tried to figure out what to do. You can't accept gifts from foreign governments for many reasons—the big ones being that it can be seen as bribery and that the gifts could be bugged—so we were good Girl Scouts and called Penny, the protocol officer. I felt, I'm not going to lie, a little excited. We were in possession of illicit jewels!

Penny explained that we had to hand over any gifts to the State Department, which would assess their full market value. We could then buy the jewels back at that price. If we didn't, they would go to auction and the proceeds would be used to pay down a debt of the government. As I did not anticipate ever having enough money to purchase those jewels, I bid them farewell. They didn't really go with my wardrobe anyway. Even back when I wore J.Crew every day.

That night, Reggie Love invited us to a (casualwear) dinner at POTUS's villa. It was a huge relief after the stressful day, and I thought I'd be able to let my guard down, by which I mean complain relentlessly. As soon as I walked in I started spouting off about how insane Saudi Arabia was. "Do they *think* we weren't going to *notice* that the grass is *fake*!"

I wasn't greeted by the uproarious laughter and agreement I'd expected. Everyone looked gravely concerned. "ALYSSA!" someone hissed at me, as the others made exaggerated cut-it-out motions.

I didn't get it. I was just unwinding/ranting after a long day at work! Then someone pointed at the ceiling and I got it: They were probably listening to us.

SO HERE'S THE THING…

As VJ and I were walking back to our villas, we got confirmation when we saw the doors open and Saudis emerge from both. VJ was incensed. "Excuse me! What's going on?" They ignored us and kept walking.[1]

In my room I tried to figure out what they'd touched, to no avail. After that, we couldn't sleep, and we were emailing each other until I found an *Ally McBeal* marathon on TV—not dubbed in Arabic, weirdly—and decided to watch it separately. I was still awake for the call to prayer at 4:00 AM, which became surreal, beautiful background music to the dancing baby.

Later that year, we went to China. At the hotel in Beijing, Secretary Clinton, Huma Abedin, VJ, and I were the only women on the top floor with POTUS. I was in my room for about twenty minutes before I got a knock on the door from Secret Service: Secretary Clinton had taken a shower and noticed that the mirror was covered in steam except for one spot in the middle. They couldn't be certain, but they thought it was a camera, so they wanted me to be aware. This being a new hotel, which the Chinese had encouraged

---

1 Something similar, but with a little more slapstick verve, happened in Russia: Our first trip there—also during our first year—coincided with Michael Jackson's funeral, and Mel Winter and I asked if we could skip the Moscow event to watch the memorial service on TV. POTUS and FLOTUS didn't get it, but they also didn't care, so they said sure. We were in the middle of watching Mariah Carey belt "I'll Be There" when the door to the room opened and in walked a set of FSB agents looking…exactly like FSB agents. They must have assumed everyone was at the event, but if they were surprised by our presence in the room, they didn't look it. In fact they didn't acknowledge our presence at all; instead they just made a casual loop and walked out.

us to stay in, we already had a "security understanding" that it was probably bugged. But it was still a jolt to see what seemed like evidence of it. I showered in total darkness because I didn't want the Chinese government to see my naked body. I almost broke my teeth getting out of the shower.

What the Chinese government would do with a video of me showering is not immediately obvious. Maybe blackmail. (Luckily I don't think the leak of such a video would do my reputation irreparable harm—the impulse to share TMI can also be self-protective. Though it's possible that I shower in a really weird way that would be humiliating for the public to find out about. I have no idea. I'm not a bad singer!) But the point is that I was taking a lot of things for granted. Part of this was my American bravado and ignorance—we thought we didn't spy on people, but of course we do—and part of it was that being actively spied on (as opposed to merely having your every move tracked on your iPhone) is a strange experience. Of course, few people are being monitored to the extent that high-level government officials are. (Not that the current administration seems to heed this truism at all.) But more generally, it drove home for me how random things you do without thinking in a foreign country could change the course of your trip.

◆ ◆ ◆

It's not just officials who are tracking your every move,

either; whenever you're a representative of the US government, the public is desperate for you to do something deliciously bad that they can be righteously outraged about. Does that mean you should do something deliciously bad? No. But people do.

The trip to the Summit of the Americas in Colombia in April 2012 coincided with the middle of my gradual descent into total exhaustion. (This would eventually lead to my leaving the White House in 2014.) Since April was far enough away from the moment the campaign reached peak intensity, I was able to skip Cartagena in order to take a two-day vacation to Palm Beach with DK (now my husband). What could go wrong?

We were about to dig into our key lime pie at Morton's Steakhouse when I got a call from Clark Stevens, who handled crises. I knew immediately that I couldn't ignore it—the fact that he was calling me meant we had at least a potential crisis going on—so I went outside, sat on the curb, and called him back. I came to understand that several members of the Secret Service had hired sex workers, whom they brought to their hotel, where they were required to sign them in as guests, despite this being a blatant violation not only of agency protocol but also of common sense. Later the officers involved claimed that they didn't realize they were bringing prostitutes to their rooms, but the fact that the women were sex workers is not particularly relevant: The president was about to arrive for the summit, and bringing any stranger who might be potentially hostile to the US, with some ulterior motive, was an obviously dangerous thing to do. As Susan Collins put it during the investigation: "Who were these women? Could they have been members of groups hostile to the United States? Could they have planted bugs, disabled weapons, or in any other [way] jeopardized the security of the president or our country?" Yes, some of the agents were married. But more importantly, they all had guns in their rooms. Which the American people were soon to point out.

DK and I left Palm Beach the next day. A lot of us forget Obama's scandals because of what Trump gets away with every day, but at the time this was an explosive story that we dealt with for months, working with lawyers, the head of the Secret Service, and our detail leader to figure out how this could possibly happen and how to make it up to the American people so they could trust us again.

The only thing we found was that these Secret Service agents weren't thinking. At all. When you travel for work you should be on your best behavior, assuming you're being monitored at all times. Though the prospect of a free vacation is exciting, you need to remember it's not actually a vacation, and you can't let your guard down too much. But if that's too hard to remember, try this simpler version: Don't hire sex workers on business trips!

SEVEN THINGS THAT ARE ALWAYS IN MY SUITCASE

- Lint roller because, well, cats.
- A lounge outfit—as close to pajamas as I can get and still be acceptable in public—to debut in the hotel dining room at breakfast.
- Shower cap: Though this used to be standard along with shampoo, lotion, and bar soap (why is it only bar soap?!), lots of hotels don't put them in rooms anymore.
- Round brush in case I need to fix my hair. I usually blow it out hoping it will last the whole trip and it never does.
- SO MANY TAMPONS. Because you never know.
- Acetone nail polish remover wipes in case my nail polish chips. Chipped nail polish is like nails on a chalkboard to me.
- ZzzQuil to help get my sleeping back on track.

Why You Should Always Listen to Michelle Obama

At a state dinner in Tanzania, I found myself in oldest-child mode. I wanted to be the foreign ministers' favorite. The way to accomplish this, I figured, was to eat everything placed in front of me, with gusto. Now, I know what you're thinking: *Not another IBS story!* Just wait. This meal was very meat-heavy, which can be a red flag, but after a couple of tentative bites I thought everything they were bringing out was safe. Actually, not just safe—good. The goodness of the meats lulled me into a false sense of security. I was chowing down, gesticulating wildly at the person next to me, one of the most interesting people I met on our travels, Dr. Asha-Rose Migiro, who had just returned from a post at the UN and was the first woman in Tanzania to be sworn in as minister of foreign affairs. Then I happened to glance across the table and see FLOTUS with a grave and foreboding look on her face. Directed at me. I paused my treatise on the Great Migration in the Serengeti to try to figure out what was going on. Squinting a little, frowning subtly so that she'd see I was trying to communicate telepathically with her without letting my confusion alarm any of the foreign ministers, I mouthed the word "What?" She began shaking her head.

When Michelle Obama is discreetly shaking her head at you, stop whatever you're doing. It doesn't matter if you have no idea what she's referring to; she's always right. But I thought she was talking about the meat. And unfortunately I became a little defensive. There was nothing wrong with the meat. By that point I was an expert at determining if food was bad, and this meat was not bad. This meat was delicious! As I was performing this cross-table pantomime, trying to defend the succulent lamb I'd just devoured, a waiter presented me with a warm towel that I used to wipe the succulent lamb juice off my hands. And, possibly, that I dabbed daintily around the edges of my mouth. As I tossed the used towel to the side and resumed eating, I thought I noticed a look of disappointment flicker across the First Lady's features. She had given up on me.

Well, it turns out the Secret Service had informed FLOTUS that the warm towels we'd been using to freshen up between courses were not, actually, fresh. I got giardia.

Also known as "beaver fever"—after hikers at Banff National Park became ill from drinking stream water contaminated with giardia from beavers—giardia is a parasite. Symptoms usually appear one to three weeks after you've encountered it. I was in so much pain I genuinely thought I had appendicitis or a rupturing ovary, and I spent most of that time sprawled out on the floor of our house in Georgetown like one of those chalk outlines at a crime scene on *Law & Order*. Now I'm always conscious of what unexpected items might be carrying contaminants and how travel disaster can strike when you least expect it.

DAN PFEIFFER ON HOW PLATONIC LIFE PARTNERS HELP YOU AVOID CATASTROPHE

In addition to his long list of professional accomplishments, Pfeiffer holds one of the most esteemed honors in politics: being my platonic life partner (PLP). Since I've benefited from his advice and companionship for years—he introduced me to Angry Birds—I asked him to dispense some wisdom on friendship (aw!) for my book.

As the custodian of my IBS secret during our trips with POTUS, you were perhaps too aware of all my digestive crises. Was there ever a time you really didn't think I was going to make it?

There is no human walking the planet in whom I have more confidence. I always knew you had a plan for all situations, including and especially emergency access to the toilet. I was a LITTLE worried your long-awaited meeting with the pope might have been a little too long awaited...if you know what I mean.

Be honest: What's the most annoying thing I've done on a trip, foreign or domestic?

This question is a trap, and I will not fall into it.

What's the closest you've ever come to causing an international incident on a foreign trip?

Hmm...there was the time I almost threw my wine at the South Korean trade minister during a dinner in the presidential palace when he decided to share his opinions with you about unmarried women in their thirties, which you were at the time.

Who are the top five most interesting people you met while working for POTUS?

The pope, the Queen of England, Magic Johnson, Kanye (the old Kanye, not MAGA Kanye), and Muhammad Ali.

Can you confirm for everyone that David Beckham was making eyes at me the night we had dinner with the queen? What's your favorite memory from that night?

There was no doubt that David Beckham had his eye on you. I know this because you told me approximately thirty-eight times that night, and once every few months (including in this question) in the seven years since. For all the Beckham talk from that night, I have a strong memory of you cornering Colin Firth and talking to him about Love Actually, which he was more than happy to discuss (seriously).

What makes me a good PLP? When did you know we'd be pals for life?

This is a hard question to answer because everyone is different, but I think the key to any lifelong friendship/platonic partnership is trust. Not just trust that someone will keep your secrets, but trust that they won't judge you in your most vulnerable or needy moments. So many friendships and relationships are centered around an ideal image that one wants to maintain—the cool one, the calm one, the strong one—but that's not how life is. You need to feel 100 percent comfortable putting down your guard and being your most authentic self, even when it contradicts the person you want people to think you are.

I always tell people that you saved my life literally and figuratively. Literally by getting me to a hospital in an Uber when I had a blood vessel constricting blood flow to my brain, and figuratively because I never would have survived two years on a presidential campaign and six years in the White House without having you there to give me advice when I needed it, make me laugh in the dark times (personal and professional), and give me a swift kick in the ass when I was being dumb. If I hadn't been willing to share with you my most embarrassing moments, my greatest fears, and my craziest insecurities, I wouldn't have made it. You never once made me feel bad or embarrassed about my darker moments. No one could ever ask for a better friend.

"How Do I Get to Be You by the Time I'm Thirty-Five?"

What are gut feelings, and how do you use them? We all want to know the secret to success, and we all want the secret to be "It's really easy, actually." So when we see someone we consider successful, we immediately think they can tell us the one easy trick to becoming successful ourselves. But the truth is it's very hard. Or at least it was for me. Too often, advice is understood to mean "telling other people what to do." But beyond "life hacks," good advice is entirely situational. Don't get me wrong—I love a good hack. (The thing Sophia Amoruso says about wearing a tampon when you go commando—life-changing.) But you can't hack your way to a fulfilling career.

Nevertheless, as my career has developed and become more "public-facing," young people approach me asking for advice. The way they phrase it is usually something like: "I want to be you by the time I'm thirty-five."

I'm sorry—I know it's well meaning. But "I want to be

[insert renowned other person] by the time I'm thirty-five" is the worst way ever to approach your life. I would not have been me by the time I was thirty-five if I hadn't been open to random opportunities that presented themselves unexpectedly. I would not have been me by the time I was thirty-five if I had a list of characteristics and accomplishments that I thought defined who "me" was.

The message I wanted to get across in *Who Thought This Was a Good Idea?* was that there's no path, and even if there were, you certainly don't have to follow it. To me, an instinct is a good way to balance what you need to do with what you want to do. You may feel pulled in one direction or another, but deep down you know what's right. When you have to consider both your dreams and your nightmares, your passion and practicality, practicality usually wins out, until it doesn't have to anymore.

No one can do what I did by being safe, and you can only take risks if you're relatively financially independent. Every component of good decision making—risk taking, trusting your gut, setting priorities—is contingent on your ability to take care of yourself. Even if we look at industries we think have clear, step-by-step procedures for reaching a senior position—investment banking, say—women rarely have opportunities to make it that far. Women are 18 percent less likely than men to get a promotion to management level, and from there their numbers in senior positions drop.

This is scary, but it's also exciting. You can't figure out how to get where you want to go without first figuring out where that is. "Success" is not a place. "Success" is everywhere and nowhere at once. It means wildly different things to different people.

Here is my trajectory, in more or less chronological order from around age fourteen, for proof:

Babysitter; bagger at Kilmer's IGA; cashier at Del's Dairy Cream; cleaner at the Beekman Arms hotel; hostess at the Beekman Tavern; babysitter; unpaid intern for Rep. Bernie Sanders; hostess again; audio transcriber for Ed Garvey, a progressive icon who unionized the NFL; babysitter; congressional intern for Rep. Bernie Sanders; babysitter again; real estate paralegal; secretary at Merrill Lynch (for five days); assistant at a very random start-up company; client relations person at Sotheby's; all-around staff assistant for John Kerry; babysitter; associate at a Republican lobbying firm (I can explain!); press secretary for Democratic congressman Rick Boucher (from Virginia's Fighting Ninth!); director of scheduling on John Kerry's presidential campaign; adviser (and then political director) to Senator Barack Obama; lots more with Obama; White House deputy chief of staff for Obama; chief operating officer at Vice Media; *New York Times*–bestselling author; president of global communications for A+E Network; podcast host; and now…TBD.

I don't think anyone would be able to make the connection between bagger at the grocery store and assistant to the president of the United States. But a lot of the skills and behaviors I developed doing odd jobs and grunt work have been useful. What will probably help regardless of your age and desired career: diligence, humility, and perspective. In every job, I tried to keep my head down, do good work, and own up to mistakes when I made them. I learned that not because someone had to tell me—doesn't it seem a little obvious to see it written down?—but because all the people I admired worked in the same way. For all his rhetorical genius and charisma, Barack Obama wasn't showy; he wasn't constantly calibrating how an action would or would not make him appear. The same was true of all my previous bosses and mentors.

Of course mentors are wonderful. What I'm saying is that you shouldn't be emulating them; you should be learning from them, taking what they can teach you, and applying it to your own life. Because not only are people different (duh), but the world changes rapidly, so what worked for me as a twenty-six-year-old in 2002 is not going to work the same for you as a twenty-six-year-old in 2019. For the first many years of my work life—note that this is different from "career"—offices were hierarchies. Lunch was never free, and neither was the coffee.

If you had an office, you were important. If you had a big office, you were even more important. And if you lived in a cubicle, your cube-mates were your only peers.[1] I spoke freely to my cube-family, but in the hallways, when passing partners or other senior-level people, I didn't strike up a

---

1 Today, I know I work well in an open-plan office; I can still focus clearly on what I need to be doing and welcome the occasional interruption from a colleague. Some people are more easily distracted. If you're that kind of person, or have ADD or ADHD, then a job in an open-plan office may be a real problem for you. Don't be afraid to consider that if you're picking among job offers. If you don't have the luxury of avoiding an open plan, don't be afraid to ask your boss about ways to limit distraction.

conversation or ask about the weather—I cheerfully said, "Hello, Mr./Mrs. Whatever!" Yes—I only called them by their first names once they said it was OK.

In some ways, it was very restrictive. The boss could torture you with whatever he—and it was always a he—wanted. But in other ways at least you knew what the fuck was up—what the power structure was, whom you needed to impress (or at least pretend to be interested in). Back then, the path to promotion was very clear, and while it wasn't kind to women, you knew what all your bosses had done to get where they were. In a post-corporate era, things can be tricky; when offices are open concept and leadership can be murky, it makes collaboration more fluid and easier, but it's also hard to figure out what you need to do to get to the next level.[2] Or what you need to do to avoid offending your coworkers. When I worked at Vice—which is famously "non-traditional"—if someone called me Ms. Mastromonaco I would have wondered if they needed to see a doctor. That's not necessarily fair—there shouldn't be anything wrong with assuming formality. But in that context—swarms of tattooed millennials in platform shoes talking about sex robots (for work!)—there definitely would

---

2 Doing your job doesn't usually qualify you for a raise. Showing initiative and creativity does. So if you're in a job that doesn't have a clear path to promotion, make sure to ask when you're interviewing—or just after you've been hired—what that process looks like. The answer will help you understand how you'll fit in, how you can grow, and if you should take the job at all. If the metrics are clear, great. Sometimes, you need to achieve more than your peers, and in some industries that means fierce competition. That is not for me. I know this. I like to collaborate and be a team. If it's a dog-eat-dog, every-woman-for-herself atmosphere, I can't work there.

be something off about showing up in a suit and addressing everyone like it's your cotillion.[3]

All this is kind of abstract, I know. That's both a good and a bad thing. This shift has taken place because of the internet, sure, but also because of all sorts of boundaries collapsing and re-forming. But before you get too overwhelmed, luckily there's still the same, very tangible bottom line for most people: My primary goal with work has always been to make money to pay my bills. It's awesome to be able to do something you love while earning enough money to avoid Top Ramen. But that's a privilege, one that has to be earned. Everyone has the right to a roof over their heads, food on the table, health care, and dignity. (Well, in America, they don't, but what I'm saying is that they should. Which is why I find myself drawn back to politics despite having vowed, when I left the White House, to never think about which tie a candidate should wear in a debate again.[4])

---

3 When you're getting ready for an interview, think about what you're wearing. First, you want your outfit to reflect your personality. (It's actually important! Especially, I hate to say it, if you're interviewing with a woman. But more and more men care about clothes, too.) Second, you want your outfit to reflect the vibe of the place you're interviewing at. People who showed up to Vice in suits to interview were immediately deemed suspicious not because we thought they were huge nerds but because you couldn't help wondering, *Um, did they even google Vice before they replied to the job posting?*

   For me: Navy pants and a white button-down—even if it's for Vice, it's gotta be ironed—is a foolproof, all-occasion outfit.

4 Many years ago, when I was working for John Kerry's presidential campaign, I was at debate prep camp in Santa Fe—a town I love!—and in charge of a sundry list of tasks, which included things like picking out ties that didn't "bleed" on TV as well as what you might call more "meaningful" work, like negotiating about format and helping review performance video. I think the bosses let me do some of the more meaningful work so that I wouldn't feel totally consumed by whether we should do a red or a blue tie,

Not everyone has the right to work a glamorous job of their choosing. Especially not right out of college.

◆　◆　◆

When I was about to graduate from the University of Wisconsin, I knew that I wanted to go into politics and government. My internships with Bernie Sanders were some of the most eye-opening and exciting experiences I'd had

---

but I appreciated it, because not everyone was so nice. One day I walked into the prep just before JK was coming down, and someone quite senior came over to me. He said, without salutation or smile, "Sharpen these," and thrust about ten pencils into my face. No "please," no "thank you," no camaraderie-forming cute joke about how old-school No. 2 pencils are.

My job was to support the team. So I sharpened the pencils.

But I never forgot that guy. Fast-forward about eight years, and I found myself working with this person again, only this time I had the power. I'd been promoted before he came into his job there, and although we were mostly peers in the White House, in a few areas I was his designated superior.

How delicious.

I'm adept at passive aggression, but this time I just went for it. I knew I'd never get past it and be able to work productively with him if I didn't say something. "Oh my God, hi!" I said when we sat down for our first 7:30 AM meeting in the chief of staff's office together. "Remember when you made me sharpen your pencils in Santa Fe?"

No, he didn't. I assumed he wouldn't. Because when he made me sharpen his pencils, I wasn't a person to him. I was a flunky. But he definitely felt embarrassed. Or at least I like to think so.

I'm not telling this story to get revenge—I knew he didn't mean to be dismissive in Santa Fe. But the lesson I learned from it is really important: Even though we can all be assholes sometimes, you should treat everyone like they could be your boss someday. Even assistants. Even assistants to assistants. Any time I interviewed with an assistant—or even set up an interview with an assistant—in the 1990s and early 2000s, I always sent a nice thank-you note on stationery. Now, I'm very OK with email thank-yous, but regardless: Thank them for their help and time, convey your enthusiasm for the position, and then drop the mic. Assistants are also very busy.

that didn't involve some kind of illegal substance or a jam-band soundtrack. So when the time came to apply for jobs, I sent faxes and letters to more than forty congressional offices, committees, political action committees, re-elects, campaign committees, and state offices.

Not one person responded to me.

I didn't have the luxury of time, so by early August I had to take the plunge into the wild world of headhunters and try to find a place that would pay me to do something and, ideally, provide some health insurance.

Again, rounds of rejection.

What was I doing wrong?

Well. Despite all of what I just said about there being no right way to have a career, there are, actually, quite a few wrong ways to go about it. Starting with the interviews.

When I was applying for these non-political jobs initially, I have to admit that I wasn't pumped about them. I was feeling dejected because the positions I wanted—and kind of felt I was destined for—weren't having it. I can also be a little bit of a brat in general, and this was especially true in my teens and twenties. All this was showing in my interviews. I wasn't enthusiastic; I didn't have original answers to questions I could have easily prepared for. (Even if it's true, the answer to "What most excites you about this position?" should never be "Not having to live at home with my parents.")

You may not *want* the job, but you may need the job. It doesn't have to be your dream, but you can psych yourself up on its possible positive outcomes: paying rent, getting "professional experience," paying off college loans, putting away some savings (I used my overtime at the job I eventually did get to go to Japan!), learning new software, living in a new city, meeting new people. Try to sell yourself on the upsides, so you can go in with some unforced positivity. And never act like a position is beneath you, even if it is. The moral of my story is that I wasn't being particularly enthusiastic in my interviews—I wasn't acting like real estate paralegaling was my passion, because it wasn't. Only after a few awkward "We'll call you"s did I realize that I was interviewing with people who *were* passionate about it. Well, maybe not about paralegaling, per se, but the career for which being a paralegal is an important first step. It's pretty easy to offend someone that way. It would be like if someone showed up for an interview to work at a family restaurant and said, "I mean, I don't really care about food. Or families."

So I did a little research, found some topics that I thought could be interesting to learn about, brought my curiosity to the next interviews, and asked questions. Within about a week I landed my job as a paralegal.

◆　◆　◆

Wanting to change the world as a full-time activist is a wonderful goal, but it doesn't always pay the bills. It makes sense to have long-term goals—which will inevitably get more specific as you get older—but the route you take there doesn't have to be a straight line. It probably can't be. And doing what you need to do to pay the bills doesn't have to be soul-crushing. It can have unintended positive effects, too.

All this is a lofty preamble for saying that, yes, I did work for Republicans one time. When I came to Washington, DC, in 2001, I had just finished a stint working for John Kerry in Boston. My salary was $20,500, and I augmented it with babysitting for a family named the Nemirovskys. I never could have worked for John Kerry and made what was a huge step in my desired career in politics without them.[5]

Or without my friend Amy Volpe, who let me rent a room in her apartment in Boston with three other women for five hundred dollars a month. That meant I had some money to move with. Even though I knew my salary was going to be low, after living in an apartment with a people-to-room ratio of at least 2:1 for six years, I was eager to live on my own. Right before my job with Kerry was supposed to start, I went down to DC, found a studio apartment in what was then a dodgy neighborhood, and went back up to Boston to pack my bags.

Four days later was September 11, 2001. My job working

---

5 While I can't tell you how to "be me by the time you're thirty-five," if you want to work in politics, I can tell you how I did it. I got to the White House because I only worked for people I truly believed in, except when I had to pay the bills. I got my general assistant job with John Kerry after I saw him give a speech on TV and felt that I really needed to work for him specifically. There are a lot of people who work in government who do it strategically, who latch on to politicians they think have the best shot at winning elections rather than politicians for whom they'd walk through fire. This works sometimes, but I don't think it would have ever worked for me. And I don't know how you'd be able to work as hard as you have to work, day in and day out, with no life, if you didn't really care about the mission.

on JK's political/fund-raising committee didn't exist anymore; it was going to be a long time before people were politicking or fund-raising.

So I had to get a job, and fast, because I had $950 rent to pay. Since I'd just had what I considered a great opportunity evaporate before my eyes, I wasn't amped about any of the listings I found. Still, I deployed the interview skills I'd learned from becoming a reluctant paralegal. I was maybe too good at feigning enthusiasm, because the best offer I got was for a Republican lobbying firm. It betrayed everything I believed in. In some ways, it was reprehensible. Maybe reading this, you still think it's reprehensible. But it paid the bills, the people were very nice, and in the end what I was doing was not specifically evil. My job was to attend trade shows and get businesses to join our organization— the American Beverage Institute—lobbying for the rights of beer, wine, and liquor companies.

I wouldn't and couldn't have stayed very long—my heart wasn't in it. But I got a very good bonus, because I was deeply grateful for the job. It paid my bills and allowed me to put some money in savings for the first time ever, which allowed me to eventually apply for another, lower-paying job in politics that I actually wanted to do. Even though it seemed like the totally wrong track, it actually got me back on track. And in the after-hours, I spent a lot of time reading and introducing myself to people who would help me get where I ultimately wanted to go.

Something kind of similar happened when I left the White House. I was so burned out on the fighting and compromising that I thought I never wanted to see or hear about politics ever again. I wanted a fun job with less stress, better pay, and nice benefits.

Everyone said I was crazy. The safest thing to do would have been to go and join a consulting firm and cash in on what I knew best: politics. But the idea made me cringe. My gut said not to do it. I knew I was young enough to start an entirely new career, that my skills were transferable, and that I had more chapters of life left to live. So after months of languishing on the couch with reality TV, going to meetings that were a little aimless at the beginning, I took the job at Vice.

I won't lie: It was hard to go from having daily conversations with the president of the United States to laborious debates about getting rid of the cold brew in the office kitchens because it was too expensive. But that's life! Every job has its challenges. I wanted—and needed—something new. I couldn't compare the two. And having to ask a twenty-four-year-old how to log into TweetDeck was an eye-opening experience.

I'm proud that I lived my dream of having a career in politics, and I'm proud of the work we accomplished with Obama. But I'm almost prouder that at forty, I was able to throw caution to the wind, take a risk to my rock-solid reputation in politics as an overachiever, and move to an industry that was totally alien to me, where I would be the one asking questions, not giving answers. Actually, two industries, because after I left Vice I went to A+E, and the only thing I knew about TV was that I loved to watch it.

Even if I won't be working in digital media or linear television again—as I write this, it's a couple of months after I left my job at A+E because I couldn't sit out of politics anymore—I can now say I'm conversant in both. And who knows what the hell I'll be able to do with that? (I'm hoping something extremely rad.) So far I've been mainly using it to be funny—yes, I am funny—on podcasts and rant about Trump on MSNBC, but this, I'm sure, is just the beginning. Maybe one day I'll be funny in real life. (Kidding. I'm hilarious.) Would I have ever seen myself as a successful commentator before? No. But the point is that things change, times change, and you will change. A shift in perspective is almost always a good thing.

MY FAVORITE WHITE HOUSE MEMENTOS

- West Wing parking placard: On mornings when I was mentally present, I couldn't help but be in awe driving through those iron gates every morning. Also, I was in charge of who got to park on West Exec, which was a huge pain in the ass—everyone clamoring for spots—and keeping my parking pass reminds me to be grateful that I don't have to do that anymore.
- My to-do lists: They remind me of how productive I can be when it's really necessary. Also, they are funny.
- A German Christmas music box I got in Dresden, to replace the one I broke when I was a toddler.
- Can't Get Right: This is a stuffed owl with a busted wing and crossed eye the advance team brought me from a trip to Madison, Wisconsin. Dey—Danielle Crutchfield, director of scheduling and my right-hand woman—named it Can't Get Right, and when anyone would annoy us we would make weird owl noises and hold up Can't Get Right.
- My business cards.
- Two photos: one of me on Air Force One headed to Iraq in a sandstorm, surrounded by dudes, and another of me pretending to be a hedgehog to make POTUS laugh.

Quitters Sometimes Win

Quitting fucking sucks. It doesn't matter if you've loved your job or hated it—change is hard, and no one likes being destabilized, unsure of what's going to happen next. Gone are the days when you were selling fudge at the Dutchess County Fair and felt so overwhelmed by your hatred for it that you sent your best friend in to quit for you. (You know who you are!)

No: Most of the time, how you leave a job matters as much as how you come into a job. Social media and the general lack of privacy we have now mean that your potential employer can talk to your past employer easier than ever, and your reputation can precede you more than you anticipated. Even if you want a career in fashion and you're working at a plastic-supply company, you're still forming connections and generating recommendations you'll need for the rest of your life. And they often hinge on how you act when it's your time to go.

Once you start daydreaming about quitting on the reg,

you're in the danger zone. (The same is true of relationships: Once the idea of a breakup comes to you, and you imagine yourself sipping cosmos with the girls on a singles' vacay, it's hard to turn back.) When I've gotten to that point, I'm usually bored, annoyed by coworkers, exhausted, no longer interested in the mission of the company/organization, and probably already looking elsewhere.

When I left the White House, a mission so much greater than I could ever really wrap my brain around, it was because I was depleted. It took me a long, long time to recognize this. How could I get sick of that mission? It was the mission of the *United States of America*! Slowly but surely, though, I was becoming the person I found annoying: the person who could explain in painful detail all the solutions that had been tried before and why they all failed. A combination know-it-all/hater.

If you've never reached your breaking point with a job, you're probably thinking, *Isn't that a good thing? You can anticipate problems!*

Not really. I wasn't being productive. If you're trying to find new and interesting ways to communicate what the intentions of the president's policy proposals are in a burgeoning era of "new media"—that's what we called it back then—you have to be willing to try new things, think out of the box, and fail before you hit it out of the park.

Back in 2014, for example, when we were brainstorming ideas for reminding people about the open enrollment period for the Affordable Care Act, VJ and Pfeiffer wanted POTUS to appear on *Between Two Ferns with Zach Galifianakis*. I was so against it. "This isn't 'presidential'!" I cried, scowling at my desk. From our deeply uncomfortable vantage in the Trump era, you can LOL all day long. But back then I felt I was in the right. Presidentiality was important. It was an institution. It was continuity. Never mind that *Between Two Ferns* was hugely popular and hilarious. I had no idea what it was, and I wasn't about to google something so stupid.

I just checked, and today the segment with Obama has over twenty-five million views. It was one of the most successful tools for getting the word out about open enrollment.

Progress usually needs fresh eyes, and despite my love and admiration for President Obama and FLOTUS, and my devotion to the squad, which had been together for so long, I knew it was time for fresh eyes. I owed it to the man who gave me the opportunity of a lifetime and also, tbh, to the American people. I also wanted to leave on a high note, not after people got so annoyed with me that they started shit-talking my bad attitude and lack of vision behind my back. The idea of walking into a room and seeing everyone abruptly end their conversation because they'd just been saying I had been a bitch in the 8:00 AM meeting was brutal.

Telling POTUS that I had to leave—and then actually leaving, which took much longer than I thought it would—were probably two of the most difficult and emotional things I've ever done. But I wasn't wrong, and have never regretted it.

If you have a good relationship with your supervisor, tell her how you feel. It's important to not do the French exit if at all possible. If there are other positions in the company that you're interested in, talk about it. If there aren't, explain what you've enjoyed about the job, where you see your future, and why you think it's time for a change. Most decent people would rather help you land your next gig than deal with a miserable and dissatisfied grouch. (And if you threaten or even just pose quitting and your supervisor offers you a meager raise: Don't take it. If you stay, you have to recognize she called your bluff, and she owns you.)

Sometimes we quit because we can and we want to. Other times it can be more complicated. The job may become impossible because of people in the office—no judgment. Regardless, you should always have an updated résumé, something in progress where you keep track of when each position ends. Every couple of months, give it an eyeball, gussy it up, and make sure it's good to go in case you need it. I'll be totally honest: I don't have one right now. Because I thought I was hot shit and didn't need one anymore. But it turns out that even recruiters for the most senior positions will ask you for a CV, and if you don't have one, it's not going to make you look important and cool—it's just going to make you look unprepared.

And if you're already looking for a job, few things feel worse than trying to re-create your career history from scratch in a succinct, clear, and optimistic mood. Odds are if you're in between jobs, you're probably depressed and feel like shit. The last thing you want to do is pause the *Real Housewives* marathon to describe what you did as a paralegal nineteen years ago.

Things You Should Never Say to or Around Your Boss

- "How do I get to be you by the time I'm thirty-five?"
- "I want more substantive/meaningful work." (Hate to break it to you, but filing stuff is really substantive! And your boss will probably think, or say, something to the effect of: *I filed a lot of shit when I was your age. Why do you think you're better than me?*)
- "I've been in my job for a year and I want a raise." (Instead, start with your raise-deserving accomplishments, why you love your job and the company, and how you want to grow there. Then end on "I hope that we can talk about my future." I personally like to give a raise as an investment, something that says I believe in the employee and makes them want to invest in *me*.)
- "I've been in my job for a year and I deserve a raise." (No explanation.)
- "I want to manage people." (Let's talk about this. *Why* do you want to manage people? What makes you qualified to manage people? What people skills do you have? Are you diplomatic? Do you have the temperament? I have often found that people come to me and ask to manage people not because they think it's a skill they have but because they see it as the quickest way to get a raise. The

responsibility of shepherding people's careers is not to be taken lightly! Some people are solo operators, and that's a good thing! Also: Do you want to manage people just because it's a power thing?)

- Don't tattle on other people to your boss unless someone is being a real problem.
- Don't comment on outfits your boss is wearing.
- Don't talk about your boss on social media. Even if he seems like the most Luddite manager ever, he will see it.

Ted Chiodo's List of Words AM Uses That You Should Pay Attention To

Things on the 2007 Obama campaign could get crazy. Very crazy. As the director of scheduling and advance—SkedAdv—I was responsible for a matryoshka doll of schedules: My staff was my responsibility, and their responsibilities were other people's schedules, which were also my responsibility, and the compatibility (or not) of all those schedules together was also my responsibility. Because of all the pressure, I had to be particularly careful to act like the kind of manager I'd want to have, not the kind I'd complain about with the rest of my coworkers at the bar. And that means restraining yourself and treating your employees with respect even when they make you want to tear your hair out.

So, like many managers, I came up with some ways to communicate that allowed me to express my feelings without taking them out on my employees. I'm not saying I was passive-aggressive—I loved them—but it was...reservedly tactful. Yeah. All bosses will get exasperated and drop their own version of these occasionally, but if you find yourself on the receiving end of phrases like this frequently, you probably need to shape up.

Because I spent so much time with my team, they eventually cracked my code. Which led to Ted Chiodo, whom I'd worked with since 2003, back when he used to wear pants with lobsters on them to answer the phones at Kerry campaign HQ, to send the entire SkedAdv team the following email. Edited lightly for grammar—no offense to Ted. Or TED, as he refers to himself in this dispatch:

8 WORDS OR PHRASES THAT TED CHIODO SHOULD PAY ATTENTION TO WHEN USED BY HIS BOSS, ALYSSA MASTROMONACO, BUT DOES NOT BECAUSE HE IS AN IDIOT

1. "Fine": This is the word used to end a conversation when TED is usually wrong and needs to shut up. Or when things are not fine and are in fact escalating out of control.
2. "Five minutes": This means, "TED, go sit back down. The thing you emailed me wasn't that funny."
3. "Nothing": This is the calm before the storm. This means something, and TED should be on his toes. Conversations that begin with "Nothing," usually end with "Fine."
4. "Go ahead": This is a dare, not permission. Don't do it, TED. DO NOT DO IT!!!

5. [loud sigh]: This is not actually a word, but a non-verbal statement often misunderstood by TED. A loud sigh means AM thinks you are an idiot and wonders why she is wasting her time standing here and talking with TED about nothing. (Refer to (3) for meaning of "nothing.")

6. "That's OK": "That's OK" means AM wants to think long and hard before deciding how and when TED will pay for being an idiot.

7. "Whatever": "____ YOU!"

8. "Don't worry about it—I got it": Another dangerous statement, meaning something that AM told TED to do several times but is now doing herself. This will later result in TED asking, "What's wrong?" For the response refer to (3).

Electric Chocolate Cream Pie Acid Test

It was one of those parties that gave everyone a story. The occasion was Jim Messina's fortieth birthday, the location a speakeasy called the Gibson. Being a nerd living in DC, I didn't understand what a "speakeasy" was in practical terms. I thought it just meant that the bar would be like a normal bar but more expensive, 1920s-themed, and have no sign above the door.

No—it turns out speakeasies also serve very strong drinks. Or at least that was part of this speakeasy's thing. I guess that's also in keeping with the 1920s theme, but it wasn't what I was thinking about.

Everyone got completely wasted. For months I'd been relatively temperate—only a glass of wine before bed—so by three drinks I was plastered. Around 10:30—yes, PM—my friend/ex Doug showed up. He took one look at me—I don't think I was hard to find—and shook his head.

"Alyssa, you're hammered."

"I'm going to throw up!" I said this cheerfully, as if I were saying "I'm going apple-picking this weekend!"

He put me in his car and drove me home to my bathroom. While I was in there puking, he ordered a pizza. The next thing I remember is waking up on the bathroom floor next to the pizza box.

And then, despite it being a Saturday, I had to go to work. Earlier in my tenure in government, when I worked in the Obama Senate office, Friday mornings were always a little trying—Tommy (Vietor), Favs, and I could be spotted getting French toast or bacon, egg, and cheese sandwiches, and Pete Rouse would always know what we'd been up to the night before. This morning, however, was the most hungover I have ever been at work, and maybe the most hungover I'd ever been ever. Calling in sick was not an option, and even if it had been, I don't think I would have done it: Hangovers are self-inflicted, and unless you're in the hospital, you have to pull your shit together using some combination of Advil, Gatorade, and breakfast sandwiches. It helped that everyone else there was in bad shape, engaged in similar anguished muttering that went something like, "Fuck…Mess isn't open…I need McDonald's…fuck…oh my God I *did* have another drink after that…"

When I was still depressed five days later, I had an epiphany: I was too old to get that drunk.

◆   ◆   ◆

Americans have an unhealthy relationship with substances— too many people can't control themselves and binge, or restrict themselves entirely. Our gluttonous sense that bigger is better pervades everything from food to shopping, but it's particularly noticeable in our attitudes toward booze and drugs. I've always been of the belief that there's nothing wrong with moderate imbibing, and even a righteous hangover like the one I just described has its uses. It gives you valuable perspective. Your actions have consequences. Death is no longer an abstract concept but imaginable through your devastating headache and inability to stop puking. Assessing your hangovers over the years, you get the sense that age is actually more than just a number.

Nevertheless, it doesn't make much sense that alcohol is the least intimidating of the ways to chemically alter our brains. As I've already said, I've always loved smoking pot and think it should be legal and available. I wouldn't call myself a "pothead"—I never got into waking and baking, and even now I still can't roll a joint (luckily you can buy them!)—but ever since I was in high school I could appreciate the way it easily subtracted the drama from my life. When I got into it, I loved what it represented—chilling out and listening to the Dead and Phish—but I also truly felt, and still feel, that I'm my best, most creative self when I've smoked a little weed. Not completely stoned, sprawled on the couch not knowing where my arms are, but a little mellow and fluid. Vape pens helped me write this book (and with my IBS). I don't think that's something to be ashamed of.

As far as other drugs go, weed shouldn't necessarily be lumped in with them: It's not the same as, say, acid. But as we learn about the positive effects MDMA can have on people with PTSD—and I just read an article about how octopuses become sweet and loving when they're given ecstasy—and get more and more comfortable with drugs like LSD, I think it's time to admit that all drugs are different, that all people's relationships to drugs are different, and that they don't have to cause life-ruining experiences. Particularly if we started a genuine conversation about how to use them responsibly, rather than issued grave warnings that always end up making people curious instead of scaring them away.

So I'm going to tell you about the one time I did acid, which was actually very wholesome. I was always interested in it because the musicians I liked did it; I looked up to them, and they always said it opened their minds. I agree that it opens your mind (if you take the right amount), but to fully take advantage of that, you have to be the kind of person who channels your creative energies into something in the moment instead of lying on the floor staring at the ceiling and laughing. As you'll see from this story, I'm a combination of both.

I took a quarter tab at a friend's house and had planned on spending the night, but things took a turn when I started feeling it and decided I needed to locate one of my ex-boyfriends from high school, Jon. Well, Jon was never really my boyfriend-boyfriend; he was a year older than I was, a farmer, and always smelled like soap. I'd thought he was funny; maybe I was reminded of him because once I was on acid I couldn't stop laughing, to the point that my face and stomach were sore the next day.

I maintain that I was not pining for him—I was just inspired to seek out a spiritual reconnection. My buddies all felt very strongly that this was an impulse I should follow through with. But what form would my communication with him take? I thought and thought. And then somehow I'd written an epic poem. I didn't sign it because I thought at the time that my essence would shine through in the writing. In retrospect, maybe my sober subconscious was looking out for me.

The delivery of the poem quickly became a group project. One of our (presumably amused) friends had been designated the sober watcher, and we conveyed our desperate need for her to drive us to his house. It would be an epic journey for an epic poem! I think part of her job was to go along with our whims provided they weren't harmful to ourselves or others, so she agreed. Overcome with our sense of our own generosity, on the way to Jon's house we realized we needed to stop at Grand Union market to buy several chocolate cream pies that we would leave on people's doorsteps, including one for Jon. She also complied with that request. (Well, it was more of a demand.) When we reached his house I included my poem on top of his chocolate cream pie and skipped back to the car, laughing hysterically at the beauty of it all.

I never heard from him, and I didn't care. But fast-forward to November 2013. No longer am I a free-spirited college student with an Eddie Vedder haircut and a basic knowledge of Japanese but a newly married woman with a sick cat, an impressive political career, and a basic knowledge of Japanese. While DK and I were visiting my family for Thanksgiving in Rhinebeck, our cat Shrummie had a stroke, so we went on another epic journey, though this time my mind was only altered by years of exhaustion and frantic concern about my cat.

We were sitting in the waiting room at the vet when I heard the doctor say to a nurse, "Mastromonaco...I think my husband went to high school with her." It was Jon's wife. She helped Shrummie get back on his feet. I got them and their kids tickets for the Easter Egg Roll at the White House. Though none of us ever mentioned the poem, or the chocolate cream pies, I like to think that acid—ingested responsibly, with supervision preventing physical and social catastrophe—had something to do with the feelings of warmth and goodwill shared by all.

The Woman in Red Leather Pants

In the days leading up to Sally Davis's[1] twelfth birthday party, there was a lot of whispering in the lunchroom. Those of us invited—which included people like me, as well as some of the popular girls, who, in a coup for Sally, were known to be attending the party—were specifically privy to the rumors. Most of us knew where they were coming from: none other than Jessica Laramie, Sally's best friend. Instead of seeming like a red flag—why would Sally's best friend want to spread rumors about her?—this only made the gossip seem more credible. But ultimately the whispers were too suggestive to mean anything to our twelve-year-old brains other than: intrigue!

The gossip didn't come to a head until the actual party. All us girls were sitting at Sally's house, in her front room. We'd dropped off our presents in a pile for her to open

---

1 Not her real name. "Jessica" was not *her* name, either.

later. My gift was a Rick Astley tape; I loved Rick Astley and likely had the same one at home. Everything was going well until Sally left the room for some reason. It was then that Jessica decided to drop her bombshell. "I figured out what's wrong with Sally," she said conspiratorially. For me, and I'm sure for many of the other girls present, the only indication that something was wrong with Sally had come from Jessica. But Jessica's confidence in stating it meant we all had to pretend that we'd noticed something wrong with Sally, too. Because we were impressionable middle-schoolers, this quickly morphed into us thinking there actually was something wrong with Sally.

"She's a *lesbian*."

Everyone in the circle was shocked. Jessica had been talking smack before, sure, but it was only here, at the actual party, that she had dared use the word "lesbian."

"Yes," Jessica continued gravely. "She's...*that way*."

The evidence? Sally had sleepovers, and at the sleepovers girls would sleep in the same bed.

Which, by the way, is typically what happens at sleep-overs. But the seductive power of the gossip was greater than the steady force of logical reasoning.

Now, before I get into my (shameful) involvement in this story, let's unpack the motivations at play here. Sally had invited popular people to her birthday party, and they attended. Jessica wanted those girls to be her friends, so she started telling people that Sally liked girls in order to make us uncomfortable and not want to be around her. This also doesn't make much sense, except when you remember that popularity in school doesn't work the same way it does in adulthood. In adulthood the seas often rise together; that's what networking is all about. Your friend moves up a level, and you suddenly start getting +1 invites to fashion shows. In school it's more of a zero-sum game: Some people are chosen, and their friends get left behind. Jessica saw Sally's possible ascent as immediately threatening to Jessica's own prospects.

Like most of the other girls in the room—I won't speak for everyone!—I was overtaken by a vague but potent outrage when I heard that Sally was (allegedly) a lesbian. At the first opportunity, I snuck over to the present table and took back my Rick Astley tape. When I got home I threw it in the trash, to really establish my conviction that she didn't deserve a present.

A few hours later, though, I began to feel bad. Was Sally really a lesbian? And if she was, what would be wrong with that? She hadn't done anything but invite a bunch of people to her house and feed us cake and pizza.

I'm pretty sure Sally never knew what happened that day, thank God. To this day, she has no idea she missed out on a sweet Rick Astley tape because of stereotypical Mean Girl posturing. Because we were all mostly good people, the angels on our shoulders eventually prevailed, and the gossip didn't circulate beyond the party. For days afterward, I thought about how sad I'd be if people said things about me that weren't true. (I still get upset about mild professional rumors I hear about myself—and I'm talking really mild.) I think I've always understood that anything I hear about extremely personal aspects of other people's personal lives—illness, divorce, pregnancy, and other potentially devastating topics—shouldn't be spread. But this taught me that the reverberations of gossip can continue even if nothing actually comes of it.

◆ ◆ ◆

This is not going to be a complete lecture about the evils of gossip. And I'm not going to chastise anyone for engaging in any version of it at all. Of course gossip happens. It happens a lot. It can be fun and harmless. When I worked in politics, where tensions are always high and people are always having affairs, gossip was particularly rampant. We all enjoy a good gossip session, and often, it can be harmless—a way to let off steam, to compare notes. You can even learn something from gossip. The kernels of truth are usually there. (Though not always—and you can't afford to assume.) Sometimes, gossip even works as a way for those with less power to work around those who have more and may be using it unfairly. And gossip as an adult is obviously very different from the ruthless rumor-mongering most of us engaged in in school. Adults are savvier, more careful with their secrets. (Well, sometimes. Sometimes they're much, much less careful.) But as you age, the stakes in gossip get higher and higher: In school, everyone is more or less immature and not expected to know any better. You also know everyone will eventually graduate and move on. But there's no designated start-over point in life. The motivations—and consequences—behind gossip are always worth thinking about. If someone's gossiping with you, it makes you feel like you're in an inner circle. Most of the time it doesn't occur to us that someone could be saying the same kinds of things about us on the other side of town. And with social media, you can morph into a twenty-first-century Nancy Drew and put all the pieces together to confirm the story you've developed in your head.

So the question is not "How can I stop gossiping?" It's "How can I gossip responsibly?"

Some basics: Know when you should receive the gossip but not perpetuate it. If someone wants to tell me something, that's fine—sometimes it's more than fine; it's delightful—but I try not to repeat it. If I do repeat it, I'm taking a risk, but I try to minimize the risk by repeating it to trustworthy people. (That I was considered a trustworthy person to the original person in possession of gossip is part of the point. Things can easily get out of hand!) Ideally, the people you tell could be helpful in the situation, or they might need to know. But of course that's an idealistic framing; you may have some friends who exist entirely for the purposes of gossiping together. That's not bad, per se, but it is worth thinking about when it comes to serious pieces of information. Because there's also a big difference between gossip and secrets. Sometimes people will come to you to get something off their chest or to ask for advice; turning that moment of vulnerability into an opportunity for petty self-advancement, or a quick hit of conspiratorial camaraderie, is cruel.

When you're participating in rumor-worthy behavior, you also have to be very, very careful, because gossip works in sneaky ways. Even the most insignificant-seeming action can trigger the alarm. On the Kerry campaign, for instance, there was a rumor that a married man was having an affair with an attractive younger woman. Everyone would gossip about it, but I assumed it wasn't true—just an example of heightened nerves driving speculation. I was in charge of hotel rooms back then, and we didn't have a big travel agency (since it was the beginning of the campaign) and I'd call the hotel to confirm everything was copacetic with the check-in process. On one trip, I called the Holiday Inn or wherever it was, and the receptionist informed me—just as part of protocol—that the attractive younger woman hadn't checked into her hotel room.

Even if you suspected it was true, there's always a moment of shock when you learn that gossip is not just rumor but rooted in reality. It was right in front of your face all along! As soon as the receptionist said that, I knew the attractive younger woman was involved with the married man. She had definitely been on the trip.

This gossip had real consequences: her reputation, his marriage. (And his reputation.) It was none of my business, but I sent her a polite, non-judgey note to say, "Hey, just FYI, be a little more scrupulous in the future." I wasn't scolding her; I believe it's fine to have an affair. (I mean, not *fine*, because it causes a lot of pain, but it happens all the time. Regardless, none of my business, and certainly nothing that should come up if it's not affecting either party's work.) But if she didn't want other people to know she was having an affair with a married man, she should be more careful! Ditto with social media: It's public. People can see who you're friends with, what posts you "like," and increasingly they can even see when you're online. This intersects with the workplace in a way it didn't in the past: Making your account private doesn't really help—it's hard to justify not accepting people you see every day. That means they're going to know stuff about you.

◆　◆　◆

I think I've established how dysfunctional the Kerry campaign was, here and elsewhere. Well, it's possible I was a gossip angel during that time period because I knew how it felt to have your personal life dissected behind your back. On the Kerry campaign, everyone was saying my boyfriend was cheating on me. And he was!

The revelation came thanks to a series of technological loopholes. Many of you won't remember this, but in the BlackBerry era, you used to have to empty your email inbox when you had between four hundred and five hundred messages. You could only accomplish this online, on a desktop. (No wonder nobody's using them anymore. But I'm still a fan.)

Doug didn't have a laptop on the road, so sometimes he'd call me and have me dump his inbox for him.

He must have trusted me a *lot*. Of course I abused his trust. But of course he was abusing my trust first, and in a worse way, so here we are. If you feel you have to read your boyfriend's emails, you kind of already know what's in there. (For the record: It's never crossed my mind to care about my husband DK's inbox. I'm sure it's all golf and…golf…) It became a real tool for me. I'd hear from people that he'd always visit a certain woman in Iowa…so then I'd look at his emails. (It never occurred to me, though, to think about what motivated people to alert me to these visits.)

What I found was that he was receiving messages and not replying. Boilerplate sexy messages. Descriptions of outfits, expressions of yearning. I somehow learned she owned red leather pants. And she was married. Which meant, to me, that he was responding via text message or some other medium.

When he got home, I called him out on it. He was cheating on me with a married woman in red leather pants!

He just looked at me and said, "My emails are none of your business."

Was this a fair assessment? It's complicated. But it shut me up. And I stayed with him.

I know, I know. I chalked it up to the campaign being crazy and high pressure, and we all do things we regret. But I also think that the haziness of gossip allows you to delude yourself and to take things with a grain of salt. I had no *actual* proof that Doug was seeing the woman in the red leather pants—maybe he really was receiving unsolicited emails? Not likely, but certainly within the realm of possibility. Right? Right?! The fact that he'd made me a target of gossip among my team should have gotten me angrier than it did at the time. I was always the boss over people my age; "Well, her boyfriend is cheating on her" is a great way to deflate the person you're being forced to respect. When the women would say they couldn't believe we hadn't broken up, it was easy to discount them because I thought they were just taking out their resentment of me on my rumored relationship problems. I also wanted to prove the gossip wrong.

Still, after I realized his inbox was ground zero, I read his emails for months after that. (Yes: For some reason I still had access.) The straw that broke the camel's back was a message from a woman who, for some reason, thought it necessary to tell him what nail polish she got at her mani-pedi. Come on.

But that's not where this story ends! Oh no. By the time the Obama campaign rolled around, Doug and I had been broken up for years and had reestablished a great friendship. Which was good, because we both worked on the Obama campaign as well. I knew he was dating other people. I, however, was typically single. Until I wasn't, sort of. One day he heard people gossiping that I was hanging out with another guy (let's call him Joel), which made him feel like he wanted to get back together with me.

Vengeance? Not really. Instead of being an adult and saying to himself and his close friends, "She's met someone and I'm jealous," he decided he was in love with me. Soon, he was expressing this emotion to *Obama*. He and Obama were (and still are) close, and it was pretty early in the campaign, which meant he had more time for gossip. I should say, too, that we had all worked together for years at this point, and been through a lot. So a little bit of mischief was not unusual coming from POTUS.

We were all in Miami for a fund-raising trip when they—or maybe it was just POTUS—decided to implement their *Get Alyssa Back!* plan. I can't remember if Joel was there, but at one point POTUS told me to take a car with him instead of riding with the rest of the group. I said sure; also in the car were Doug, Reggie, and Julianna Smoot. As soon as the doors closed and we started to roll away, making an escape impossible, POTUS turned to me and said, in his wisest fatherly tone, "Alyssa, this is foolish. You two"—gesturing to me and Doug—"should just get back together. You're meant to be together." Smoot was cracking up and pinching my thigh as I sat there silently receiving his counsel, confused and a little embarrassed. I mean, Doug was *in the car*.

I'm ashamed to admit this, but I ended up breaking things off with Joel. I got too distracted; I reasoned that if Doug was telling Obama he wanted to get back together, he must have really meant it. Seeing me with another man was just too painful! He'd seen the error of his ways! I decided we should get back together, too.

Well, no. Of course not. Because in the final act, email makes a valiant comeback.

A girlfriend of mine was on the debate prep team, and while she was in a meeting she noticed another woman on the debate prep team messaging Doug. The friend called me and tentatively began to relay the scene. "I love you," she began, "and I know you were dating Joel, but I just thought you should know that Doug is definitely flirting with this other woman…" At first I didn't know what she was trying to say. I assured her that it was all in the past— we had only JUST decided to get back together. But then she conveyed that she was watching the flirtation happen live, in front of her at that very moment.

Soon after, I had a few drinks with my friends at a bar, and I went nuts. I couldn't wait any longer to express my displeasure. So I left my friends inside, went out into the street, called Doug, and started screaming into the phone. I can plead a little bit of campaign insanity, but I think the real moral of this story is that gossip giveth and taketh away and giveth and taketh away again. We really are better off as friends. (Which we still are.) (I swear.)[2]

---

2 This story is from many years ago, when both Doug and I were not so smart. He's now a wonderful husband and father and one of my dearest friends, who has supported me in countless ways since we broke up. For more on the inspiration for our post-breakup friendship, see page 139.

"Tell Alyssa She Needs to Get Better at Email"

I didn't start using the internet seriously until I graduated from college, and part of me still thinks it would be good to implement this as a policy somehow. You can't log on until you've been legally drinking for at least one year. That way you have personal experience with the kind of trouble you can get into on social media. Until then it's hard to understand things like recklessness, how easy it is to know something is bad but do it anyway, headaches, and the way a snap decision made in the heat of the emotional moment when several friends and strangers are screaming around you can have a lasting impact on your well-being.

My introduction to the internet was anticlimactic. We got email at UVM, but no one knew what it was good for or how to use it. All the universities used to have quirky non sequiturs in their email addresses; ours was "gnu," as in the large antelope. I knew what it was because of Gary Gnu on the '80s kids show *The Great Space Coaster*; Gary was the host of a news show and his tagline was

"Gno gnews is good gnews." My address was something like "amastro@gnu.uvm.edu." Occasional reminders from professors or the student union would pop up in my inbox, which had all the design flair of a filing cabinet, but it wasn't somewhere to camp out from the moment you woke up until the moment you fell asleep like it is now. It didn't seem like there was anything to do.

Until I discovered tape trading.[1]

As you may know, I love the Grateful Dead. I also love God Street Wine, and other jam bands you may not even be able to google at this point. I don't remember how I realized I could use the internet to facilitate this passion of mine, but I got involved in forums, where in addition to lively discussions about whom you'd met in the parking lot at Wetlands, you could request tapes. Sometimes you'd send a person a blank tape and they'd dub it for you and send it back; other times you'd trade. The borderline indecipherable lingo we used—"blistering version of '91 NYE Rhinecliff Hotel trade for tapes of any Dead shows from Autzen Stadium"— lived on the internet for many years. But every time I look at Twitter or Instagram—which is much more often than I'd like to admit—I'm grateful that my hippie passion for extended guitar is the extent of the digital residue available from my most potentially embarrassing years.

---

1 I can't believe I have to explain this, but I also know I probably have to for some of the young readers (no judgment): A "tape" is not a roll of adhesive you use to wrap presents or fix torn sheets of paper, but rather a cassette tape, a physical, post-record, pre-CD method of listening to music. Please don't tell me I have to define "CD"!

After I graduated, the internet started feeling more important. When I got a job as a paralegal in the World Trade Center, we were given email accounts and used them mainly to discuss edits on documents. It wasn't really used socially—people were pretty cautious. But as time went on they got less cautious, as people tend to do.

One day my best friend in the office, Volpe, was emailing me about "GPB," one of the lawyers who was senior to us but wasn't our direct supervisor. Volpe had a crush on him, and we were trying to determine whether he liked her back. We all thought the lawyers were sexy and important until the company instituted casual Fridays and their uniform of rugby shirts tucked into khaki pants disabused us of that myth. Weirdly, GPB's constant references to "flip and chug" didn't convince Volpe he was unworthy before. They'd been out for drinks, and he once came over to help us hang up a shelf.

The situation we were dissecting at the time was an email he'd sent her, so she forwarded it to me to ask me what I thought of its significance. I thought it was significant and I wrote back something funny.

Although we were emailing, our cubicles were so close that we could see each other; we were all grouped in an enclosed area known as the Para Pit. When we wanted/ needed to procrastinate we used to just stand up—the cubicles were like four feet high—and start gossiping or talking about movies or the news. (I think people were a lot more interesting back then—now sometimes I start talking about an article and I can tell everyone around me has only read the headline. Back in the day the headlines were not so descriptive as to lull you into a false sense of comprehension!) When I didn't hear her cackle at my joke moments after I sent it, I was alarmed.

I stood up and peered over my cube. "Volpe, did you get my last email?" I asked, already panicked. No. I checked my sent mail; of course, somehow, because of our pre-2000 technology, I had replied to GPB and not to Volpe. Crisis mode. Our friend Bama said he knew how to "recall" emails. Recall the email! Recall the email! I felt so guilty.

Turns out, he absolutely did not know how to recall the email.

Volpe was admirably calm in spite of my betrayal. Finally, the IT guys told us they managed to somehow wrench the telltale message from cyberspace before GPB could open it. But months later, Volpe ran into the lawyer in Boston, and as she was leaving he said, "Tell Alyssa she needs to get better at email." I'm pretty sure she's forgiven me, but she still brings it up.

Since then, I've been fairly relentless about my virtual communication practices, not only so that information doesn't get into the wrong hands but also so that I don't find myself annoying my friends and colleagues by wasting their time:

1. Read the whole fucking email before you respond.
2. Don't ask someone to take time explaining something you could google.
3. If you are on the "CC" line, DO NOT REPLY ALL.

EVER! If you are on the CC field, people want you to know what's going on but don't need you to make a decision about anything, so don't fuck things up by replying all with an annoying question or suggestion. Email the sender first.

4. On a group email, always direct your question to someone, or to specific people. If not, you'll end up with a long thread and no answer.

5. "Loop" me into an email chain without saying why and lose my friendship and respect forever.

6. Don't use email if you have had more than two drinks or one joint.

I also always check the "to" field and only text gossip to people I trust. I know texting isn't any safer than any other written form (except actual letters...maybe), but it's comforting to imagine I have boundaries. When all of Paul Manafort's encrypted Signal conversations were circulating because he'd backed them up on the cloud I felt a flash of something that wasn't exactly sympathy but closer to worried hypothetical identification: I could imagine the same thing happening to me. Not that I've committed fraud—I swear!—but you know what I mean: We all put things in writing that we perhaps shouldn't be putting in writing. The only real solace is that everyone has at least one bad email lurking somewhere, and if they're ever all leaked at once (this is a fear I believe many of us have) I hope I'm boring enough that no one would think to search the inevitable database they'd be in for my name.

◆ ◆ ◆

There's a big difference between the social internet and the practical internet. Both *can be* useful; the latter just doesn't come with quite so many life- and society-ruining disadvantages. But regardless, I was a late adopter—I don't think I used the internet at its maximum capability until I started working at Vice at the beginning of 2015. The catalyst was that when I got there, I still had a BlackBerry, and although I wanted to keep it, the IT guys told me I couldn't because they didn't know how to put my Vice email on the BlackBerry. How different would my life be if I still used a keypad?

Even by the time of the Kerry campaign, which was beholden to the twenty-four-hour news cycle, things that made your life easier weren't necessarily on the internet. John Kerry was a picky eater, and when he was on the road we'd have to get menus from restaurants in towns he'd be visiting so we could pre-order dinner and pick it up to save time. But restaurants rarely put menus online, so you'd have to call them and ask them to fax you the menu. Then you'd have to type up the menu (because if you scanned the faxed copy it wouldn't be readable) and send it to someone to give to JK.

Everything took so much longer, and I at least worked so much harder. Working in the press office didn't mean trawling Twitter and Facebook all day until you found something worth screen grabbing (or clicking on); you had to read every single paper, clip out the articles, photocopy them, and fax them to whoever might need them. Now you can just search a word on Twitter to see what people are saying about an issue or use Google News as a jumping-off point (as long as you understand the perspectives of each outlet you find, of course). That's why I have such a good understanding of Vermont, where I interned for Bernie, and of what was going on when I worked for JK—you couldn't find exactly what you wanted as soon as the urge struck you; you had to wade through all the news. It was active. You couldn't just sit at your computer and google until you died.

Which is what I feel like I do for work today. Now I waste more time than I have ever wasted in my life. I didn't have a personal computer until I left the White House, so the only internet I used was at work. I did some online shopping (not technically allowed) but never went much beyond that. Any new convenience the World Wide Web offered was incorporated into my life as a small perk rather than evidence of the huge cultural shift it was. Now: no. It's true that my jobs are less…essential, shall we say, than working on campaigns or for the president, but I do have a lot to do, and yet I find myself actually engaged in the process of doing it less and less. I don't mean to sound like a nostalgic old fogey when I say this, but things used to be different, and not everything is better.

When I lived in Boston and commuted to work, I'd be reading the paper on the T and someone would ask me what article I was reading; more shocking is that I wouldn't feel aggrieved that this person had interrupted my multi-tasking project of reading the news, listening to Madonna on my headphones, and texting four of my friends about the date I'd been on the night before, but happy to talk to this stranger for a few stops. And relationships with non-strangers were different, too; the people you knew were the people you'd met or heard about from your friends. Now my circle is huge but very porous; I have many levels of relationships with people, including those I've never met, but they're confusing. It's much more difficult to understand the nature of your relationship to people you've met once in person but may speak to multiple times a week in public forums like Instagram or Twitter. Whom can you trust? Who will come to your birthday party? Who will tweet something mean about you the second it seems convenient to do so?

All this confusion is compounded by the fact that the internet is not something I begrudgingly use only because it's necessary—I'm on it all the time. I attribute this to my first experience on Twitter. After I left the White House, Mindy Kaling helped me set up my account, and within a few days I was using it as God intended, which is to say monitoring barely perceptible shifts in celebrity gossip. I had accumulated about two hundred followers when one day, I saw that Mandy Moore was getting divorced from Ryan Adams. This was my chance: I knew all about Ryan Adams. I tweeted something to the effect of "yay I support Mandy Ryan Adams is terrible" and then logged off and went about my day.

About twelve hours later, I had forgotten about it. But then I checked Twitter. And he had responded! The way anyone would respond to something like that, which is to say he tweeted something like "go home, Grandma," to the mild approval of his fans.

In the grand scheme of things, this was not a big deal. But I felt totally blindsided—the idea that my reputation, even in this small, relatively insignificant way, could be morphing unbeknownst to me while I was going about my day offline gave me a compulsion. I felt like I needed to constantly check to see if anyone had said something bad about me. Which is not usually how it starts—usually you're checking for likes—but it's all part of the design.

Now, I try to keep most of my stuff positive, unless it's about Donald Trump and the crew, in which case I try to keep it extremely negative. It's a little disappointing that the negative stuff gets an exponentially bigger response— every viral tweet I've had is angry or upset—than the nice stuff, which it always seems about eight people care about. It's much easier to drum up an impassioned pack mentality about something infuriating than "This person's charity project is awesome!" Still, I always check all my mentions because I like to wade through to find the nice stuff, and to talk to people, which is supposed to be the point of Twitter, and if I'm going to use it I feel like I might as well get something out of it. When random strangers say terrible things, it's usually about my appearance—guess what, ass-holes, I know I'm not skinny!—or the fact that I have more than one cat. (What is this, 1915?) The meanest tweet any-one ever sent to me was when I thought my cat Petey went missing and tweeted a photo, to which someone replied, "Check Weight Watchers."

These kinds of insults are much easier to ignore than attacks on something I've actually said. That's why if I have a thought that's even slightly controversial—except when I'm live-tweeting *The Bachelorette*, when I shoot from the hip—I always fact-check. I have a lot of followers, which is heady and something I see as a responsibility: You see so many people tweeting out blatantly untrue or misinformed takes to hundreds of thousands of followers, and I don't want to be one of them. What Trump has done with the official White House accounts is so depressing to me and dangerous to everyone—people should always be able to look at those and see facts, not gossip or propaganda. Even if they know, deep down, that what they're being presented may not be 100 percent the truth, they haven't made the mental leap to accepting that something the White House posts online may not be true. It works on reality TV, but not with the actual news.

In other words, even though I tweet funny things—or what I think are funny things—I take social media really seriously, and I think everybody should. It may have seemed like a fun way to waste time and talk to your friends when it first started, but its power is now obvious and undeniable. You can either use it to your advantage or let it use you.

In Praise of Monica Lewinsky

I remember the fall of 1998 very clearly. I was twenty-two and living in that one-bedroom on Prince and Thompson in Manhattan that I always talk about because four of us shared it and, come on, that's pretty intense. It was some of the most fun I've had in my life. We got up early and took turns getting ready in our single bathroom so that we could all be on time for work at 9:00 AM.

At the end of the day, we'd all get home, discuss what we wanted for dinner—usually Wasa crackers with tuna and mustard, a half of a turkey sandwich from M&O's on the corner, or, if we were splurging because someone got some overtime money on her paycheck, pad thai—and then flip on the antenna TV. Regardless of the meal, we were either watching the final season of *90210* or Bill Clinton's impeachment proceedings. Only three of us could fit on the couch, so one person—usually me, not because I'm a martyr but because lying on the floor felt good sometimes—would lie on the rug. We didn't have space or money for a vacuum, so the rug had seen some things, but it was fine.

I don't mean to harp on this, but the news would play out so differently now in terms of public opinion—not necessarily in outcome—that I have to mention it: We didn't have any form of social media back then, so any news we got was usually at home, from the TV, during designated and contained time periods. Now we take to Twitter to get little hits of what's happening all day, and those concentrated dispatches aren't just straight news: They encompass a huge amount of opinion. Back in the day, Tom Brokaw or Dan Rather would give you the news, which was presented as facts, unadulterated by subjectivity. Of course, there's no such thing as pure news—any way you present something is going to color it one way or another—but it was much more straightforward than it is now. So instead of glutting yourself on what other people thought online, only to grow so sick of hearing interpretations of the day's events that by the time you get home you never want to hear another opinion again, you would usually have conversations with your friends about what you saw on TV.

The news is just as surreal now, but at the time there was much more of a disconnect between the way it was presented and the emotions it inspired. As we watched the live coverage of the hearings, we were totally glued to the TV. It was unbelievable. Did no one else think it was unbelievable? The news back then, with no slant discernible to the naked twenty-two-year-old eye, lacked all compassion or outrage. I mean, of course the Republicans were outraged—or they were pretending to be—that the Democratic president had been having an affair in the Oval Office. And of course the Democrats were outraged that Republicans would purport to be so outraged by this that they'd try to impeach the Democratic president. But there was no outrage expressed on behalf of the person who was being used as a political pawn in all this, a twenty-four-year-old woman who was being torn apart by gossip columnists, reporters, and even some feminists, who defended Clinton as a progressive savior, a twenty-four-year-old woman who was being chased, stalked, humiliated, threatened with twenty-seven years in prison, and ostracized all because she did something countless others before her had done: have an affair with her boss. Who was also more than twenty-five years older than she was and, oh yeah, the president of the United States. She described the experience in her 2018 essay for *Vanity Fair* as "a living hell."

Did the ruthlessness toward her have something to do with her strength, her refusal to be portrayed as a victim, helpless to resist Clinton's charms? Maybe. Women can't seem to do anything right. Never mind that she wasn't even the one on trial and that Clinton corroborated what she said.

I have to admit now that I myself didn't think much about Monica at the time, or as much as I should have. Her humanity, her courage, what she must have been feeling—none of that was presented in the news. To infer Monica's character from the coverage—which portrayed her as a sexually deviant temptress in a blue Gap dress, or a Valley Girl airhead in a thong—required a concentrated effort, a willingness to think critically about what was presented as fact on the nightly news. I, at least, hadn't even thought to develop that kind of skepticism. I knew she was around my age, but no one who was on TV, or working in the White House (where I wished I could have worked but didn't get a job), seemed like they could be my age. She was in another world. I remember feeling like I'd have no fucking clue what I would have done if I'd been nabbed by the FBI in the food court of a mall. General Tso's chicken never tasted the same after that. But the main thing I remember being very upset about was Bill Clinton's lying: The trial cost so many millions of dollars, and the expense could have been avoided if he'd just told the truth. All I could think about was how many homeless people could have had meals with that money.

I'm not going to give you a lesson on the nuances of impeachment because I wouldn't do it justice, but if you want to hear a fairly straight version of the events that led up to the impeachment—and the circus that ensued during and after the trial—I'd recommend listening to the Slate podcast *Slow Burn* and watching the docuseries *The Clinton Affair*. I found them riveting, and not just because they made me realize how much was unreported, or unacknowledged, at the time, and how little I could have possibly understood at twenty-two years old.

But not all women in their early twenties were clueless like me. Monica Lewinsky is proof positive of that. Something that *Slow Burn* made clear to me was that Monica had the chance to cooperate with the FBI initially, privately.

After they whisked her away from the mall food court, she found herself in a hotel room with the FBI and Linda Tripp. Tripp was her lunch date, and the older woman Monica had told about the affair; Tripp secretly recorded their phone calls, eventually handing the tapes over to Ken Starr, the (supposedly) independent counsel charged with investigating Clinton. (The one that related to Monica was Clinton's claim during the Paula Jones sexual harassment trial: "I did not have sexual relations with that woman.") She could have just told the truth about what happened with President Clinton there in the hotel room and totally spared herself so much of what came after.

And she didn't do it. Because she knew that if she did, she would end the presidency. I won't ruin the podcast for you, because you should really listen to it if you don't know the story, but suffice it to say she handled herself better than pretty much anyone else would in an hours-long interrogation with the FBI, which sounded exponentially more surreal than the trial that came after. And she made Linda Tripp, who'd betrayed her and set her up, stay and watch.

As I write this today, we're a few months away from the twentieth anniversary of the impeachment vote, and because of a beautiful and random series of events, Monica Lewinsky and I are now friends. On a personal level, she is one of the most generous, forgiving, honest, open, and hopeful people that I've ever met. As an icon—which is what she is—she epitomizes resilience, empathy, and eloquence. Before she was thirty years old, she was tormented, chased, mocked as fat, crazy, a stalker, and she had to endure this not because of anything she did but because a president lied under oath and in doing so cost taxpayers millions of dollars. We often talk about young women who are sexually harassed or manipulated as being "vulnerable," but Bill Clinton is the character in this story who put himself—and the country—in a risky position. The only thing Monica did was make it difficult for Republicans to use his idiotic mistakes as political tools.

That man has gone on to be a millionaire celebrated for his progressive and productive post-presidency, yet all these years later he cannot answer the simple question of whether he ever apologized directly to Monica or her family. It would have been reasonable for her to become a bitter, cynical person. But instead of avoiding the spotlight, which anyone in her position would be more than entitled to do, she chose to use her story—highlight it, even—to protect others from suffering as she did. She took her experiences as the "patient zero" of cyberbullying—the then-unknown Drudge Report was one of the first outlets to break news of their affair—and became one of the biggest anti-bullying advocates in the United States.

When we go for a walk or see a movie, she's just Monica. But usually once or twice someone will turn their head and do a double take and I know it's not because they recognize me. When I told my mom one day that I'd been hanging out with Monica, one of the first things she said was, "She was just a baby. She was your age."

I don't think, facing what she did, that I would have made the same heroic decision to put my country above myself.

Especially when faced with the possibility of prison. (This threat probably wouldn't have come to pass—the older men interrogating her were just using it to try to get what they wanted. But she didn't know that at the time, and she still didn't cave.) Actually, I'm pretty sure I wouldn't have. I just feel lucky that I get to learn from her bravery. Since we're the same age, I can't say I hope to be like her when I grow up. But I hope to be the kind of person who earns her friendship for many years to come.

MONICA LEWINSKY ON HOW NOT TO BE A JERK ON TWITTER

After years of guarding your privacy, you joined Twitter in 2014. What made you decide to open an account? Especially when Twitter is known to be so vitriolic.

It was actually Randall Lane, the chief content officer of Forbes *magazine, who convinced me that I needed to join Twitter. He made the persuasive (and correct) argument that it would be challenging to engage in meaningful conversations about social media when I wasn't on it publicly.*

The day I joined was memorable! I didn't know how to turn off the notifications coming to my phone, so you can imagine the chaos that erupted in my inbox after my first public tweet. Early on, I was so afraid of posting the wrong thing that I would get several people to sign off on a tweet before I sent it. And it was Lara Cohen and Rachel Dodes from the Twitter staff who encouraged me, after having known me a little while, to let my hair down a bit and show some of my lighter, more humorous side. (In other words, if you don't like my humor on Twitter, blame them!)

What do you think makes a good cyber citizen? And what are some of the worst behaviors that people engage in on social media?

Online behavior is severely challenged by what psychologist John Suler calls the online disinhibition effect: Hiding behind screens, as anonymous strangers, we take on different—often less kind—personas. The worst online behaviors are doxxing—making public where people live without their consent—and all other forms of harassment and violent threats. Then there's also the dissemination of non-consensual image-based abuse. And of course, telling anyone they should kill themselves is unacceptable under any circumstance—especially when young people are involved.

The best cyber citizens are ones who are able to bring a pause to their posts and responses. I find when I'm able to do that, I may learn something (like that people who have lost someone to suicide prefer you say "died by suicide" rather than using the word "committed") or be able to engage in dialogue so someone can help me better understand a perspective. To be a good digital citizen is also to be an upstander—instead of being a bystander and doing nothing when you see someone being cyberbullied or harassed, step in if you feel comfortable, report the situation, post a positive comment or an emoji to the target of the abuse, and even consider reaching out to that person privately to say you saw what happened and you're sorry.

Have you ever tweeted something you regret? (I mean, who hasn't?) And what would you consider your funniest tweet? (Feel free to brag!)

Most of my regrettable tweets live in my "drafts" folder, but I did, actually recently, delete a tweet I had posted where I was being incredibly snarky about a public person in the news. It was all complicated by the fact that I actually knew this person and knew his family, but I felt he had been incredibly rude about me over the years—so therefore I was justified. But I realized the tweet wasn't aligned with who I want to be. I deleted it and explained as much on the site. I also felt bad that I retweeted and commented on the cute airplane couple thread after it was revealed that the woman on the plane was doxxed and shamed following all the attention.

As far as funny tweets go: According to people's reactions, I'd have to go with my response to Marco Rubio when he tried to shirk responsibility for some remarks he'd made to an intern at Politico. My reply: "Blaming the intern is so 1990s."

What's your favorite emoji? And what emoji do you use most often?

Most-used emoji: red heart (from the cards section, not the multicolored heart section. Important distinction.)

Favorite emoji: octopus. There is just something that makes me smile about that cute li'l guy.

How Jennifer Aniston Got Me Through My Breakup

Like most people, I have problems. The problems are not insurmountable, but they're sometimes unavoidable. Like many people, I deal with them by zoning out and watching TV. I developed this habit during my freshman year of college—when I was under the impression that I was the least cool and smart person in my dorm—because my arrival on campus coincided with the debut of three major shows: *My So-Called Life*, *ER*, and *Friends*.

In my dorm, Chittenden Hall, *My So-Called Life* became a common-room event. Maybe because thinking Jared Leto is hot is an equal-opportunity pastime. Jared Leto in 1994 can appeal to all genders and sexual orientations. I made some new friends from other floors during our watch parties and slowly realized that watching a very insecure, confused, and probably depressed Angela made it easier for us to talk about similar shit.[1] *ER*, meanwhile, was the opposite

---

1   Many years later, I was at an Obama thank-you event we were hosting for
    celebrities who had done events or posted on social media for the campaign

of relatable: It was exciting and wonderful because George Clooney was exciting and wonderful. His love story with Nurse Hathaway (Julianna Margulies) was more tortured than *Romeo and Juliet.* Also, I love hospital shows because it's basically like watching WebMD: You might not admit it, but you start to self-diagnose before the first commercial break. But the show that made the most lasting impact on me—as in it triggers something besides confused nostalgia about an emotionally turbulent phase in my life or yearning for George Clooney—was *Friends.*

Friends was on Thursday nights, which was also pre-weekend party night at UVM and many other colleges. Luckily, I didn't like to go out—despite what my sparkling Twitter persona may suggest, I'm easily felled by social anxiety—so what I lost in social capital I made up for in being an expert on this show. I don't think I missed an episode.

---

in 2012. And Jared Leto was there. As we all stared at him, transfixed by his tender yet piercing blue eyes, I told the bros about his significance to my freshman-year *My So-Called Life* support group. Then I went to the bathroom. When I came back, Obama was energetically waving me over. "Alyssa, meet Jared!" I knew immediately I'd been sold out and that it was now my job to fawn over Jared and humiliate myself in front of my pals, the Secret Service, and the president of the United States while the bored star of *Requiem for a Dream* tried not roll his eyes as he nodded along politely to my blabbing. I got the exact opposite. Jared seemed genuinely touched. (Well, I think he was touched, because he kept talking to me and didn't moonwalk away.) We exchanged email addresses.

A few weeks later, Obama was debating Mitt Romney, and as usual I was at home watching with Shrummie when I checked my BlackBerry and saw an email from none other than Jared Leto. (No, I will not give you his address!) He was also watching and noticed that Obama had been mic'd on the wrong side, which meant his voice was trailing off and he didn't sound as forceful as he should. I emailed the advance team and within minutes the mic somehow appeared on the other lapel. Jared emailed me right away to say he could hear the difference. And then we got married and lived happily ever after.

Though I wasn't a runaway bride and had no iconic hair-cut,[2] I immediately liked Rachel Green (played by Jennifer Aniston), who, for all her prissiness, often found herself in the kind of scrapes I could relate to: foot-in-mouth miscommunications, imbalances between expectations and reality, and disliking things before she got to know them. A couple of years later, when it came out that Jennifer Aniston was dating Brad Pitt, a man so sexy his name is synonymous with the quality, I became obsessed.

Along with my weird attachment to her character on *Friends*, I tracked every detail of Jennifer Aniston's relationship with Brad Pitt in the tabloids I was still ashamed to read. I remember the moment I heard they were potheads and liked to smoke and go to concerts—*I* was a pothead who liked to smoke and go to concerts, too! She was so likable and relatable, yet she nabbed the Hollywood heartthrob. There were fireworks at the wedding!

But the fairy tale started to get dark in early May 2004, when the final episode of *Friends*—the most-watched episode of the decade, a huge event everyone talked about for weeks afterward—aired in front of a live studio audience. And although it ended up being a dramatic moment of romantic resolution for Rachel Green, apparently Brad didn't go. I was stricken. WHY WOULD HE NOT GO?

Was he filming? Was he sick? Or was it…something else?

---

2   If you're too young to have brought a photo of Jennifer Aniston as Rachel Green to your hairdresser, let me explain: "the Rachel"—shoulder-length, face-framing layers, with an obvious place for a clip or bobby pin—was everywhere.

Now, let me state for the record that I am well aware Jennifer Aniston does not need my concern. Intellectually, I know this.

But I cared, a lot, and maybe the amount I cared made it difficult for his absence to compute. Had America's Sweetheart been left at the altar of her *Friends* finale, like a bizarro inversion of the first episode when she appears in Central Perk frazzled and soaking wet in her wedding dress and veil?!?!?!?!

The unease passed after I watched the episode. It was so emotional! Maybe none of the other cast members' partners were there—I should have tried to find David Arquette! The cast probably wanted to take in the final moments of this life they'd lived and the world they'd created together. Yes. Maybe that was it. I'd always thought TV shows were a bit like campaigns: You work fourteen-, fifteen-, sixteen-hour days believing in what you do but not knowing if people will like it or respond to it, trying to make a compromise between the integrity of the project and its commercial viability/electability. And though the cast of *Friends* was each making a million dollars an episode by the end, so this isn't a perfect comparison, it's true that for many shows you have no job security. You can be picked up or canceled at any time. Both require resilience and loyalty. And maybe a bit of obstinacy.

Six months later, I was at Faneuil Hall in Boston watching John Kerry give his concession speech. We didn't see it coming, and it was oddly one of the best speeches I think he's ever given. (Same with Hillary—her concession speech was second to none.) (Actually, this is also true of John McCain.) Anyway, days later I was on the unemployment line in Anacostia with my friend Terry, and all I could think was that I wanted to go home and rewatch the last season of *Friends*, which I had on VHS.

Rumors began to circulate that Brad had been getting cozy with Angelina Jolie, his *Mr. and Mrs. Smith* co-star and another actress in whom I could find no fault. Shortly after New Year's, there was a picture of Brad and Jen walking arm in arm—canoodling, actually—on a beach in Anguilla—he was wearing a T-shirt that read TRASH. My fears about their possible breakup were finally assuaged.

Until a day later, when they announced their separation in this statement:

> We would like to announce that after seven years together we have decided to formally separate. For those who follow these sorts of things, we would like to explain that our separation is not the result of any of the speculation reported by the tabloid media. This decision is the result of much thoughtful considera-tion. We happily remain committed and caring friends with great love and admiration for one another. We ask in advance for your kindness and sensitivity in the coming months.

A lot of thoughts were running through my head. Yes, there was the ordinary unnecessary but inevitable concern for Jen. Was she OK? Was this just for PR, or would they really remain friends? And then there was another question nagging me and the rest of the world: WAS THE ANGIE GOSSIP TRUE?!

There was also some self-interest in this fixation.

By this point, I'd been dating Doug[3]—who shared some similarities with Brad Pitt in that he was a notable figure in DC, had been profiled by hotshot reporters, and was beloved by the ladies—for about five years. He was basically double my height, handsome, and charming. Women would openly flirt with him in front of me.

I knew it wasn't forever. Back then relationships made him feel like a caged animal. Maybe a ferret. He was open about it, and felt guilty about it, but there it was. It was the classic thing where he didn't want to hurt me, and breaking up with me would definitely hurt me, so instead he tried to mete out the hurt in tiny, imperceptible doses that he felt I wouldn't notice. If we were going to break up—and we needed to—I was going to be the one who had to do it.

Even when you know you have to do it, breaking up always seems impossible. There's no good way to start. "We need to talk"? You might as well just skip the rest— it's obvious where this is going. And when you know the guy is over it and just waiting for you to cut the cord, it's even worse. He was going to be relieved by whatever I said. There wouldn't be any effort to resuscitate this relationship, at least not romantically. No begging, though I can't

---

3   Yes, I know you know.

say I didn't fantasize about it. And although he was kind of a jerk, romance-wise, I did still want to be friends.

But then I thought about Jennifer Aniston. I know—I am a teenager. But the lesson was that it didn't have to be all reality TV screaming matches and jealousy. We could get over our issues quietly and not hate each other. If Jen could be OK breaking it off with Brad Pitt and staying friends (allegedly), then I could be OK. The eyes of the world were on her—I just lived in a one-room apartment with my bed eight feet from my oven.

In totally unprofessional form, I initiated the conversation in the middle of the workday. Since we worked in the same place, this was easy—no text-message breakup here. (Don't do this!) I got it into my head that I should do it right then, and my mental health trumped professionalism. I needed to not be alone after the conversation, and at work I had Favs and Tommy next to me in the back corner of the Obama Senate office and my friend Terry, who worked for Senator Maria Cantwell, down the hall. As I said in my last book, it happened right as they were announcing the new pope.

◆ ◆ ◆

Within days—maybe one day—the ladies had pounced. I stopped being invited to as many parties, but since I couldn't risk running into some comms intern batting her eyelashes at my ex, I spent many more nights at home than I had before (seriously, I became much less awkward after college and did enjoy going out) with music, tabloids, and yes, some pot. (This was pre–West Wing, it was OK! Well, not OK, but OK.) Also, I wore my TEAM ANISTON shirt from Kitson a lot. Then, inspired by photos of Jen with her dog, Norman, I got a cat, the formidable and irreplaceable Shrummie. Who weighed twenty-three pounds and wouldn't come out from under my chair for a while.

About a year later, I took myself to go see Jen's next movie, *The Break-Up* with Vince Vaughn, in which the two play a couple who have recently broken up but are trying to keep their apartment by continuing to live together as roommates. Though I felt she deserved to have a box-office smash, I didn't realize until we were in the middle of the movie that she was doing something metafictional: She had made a movie about breaking up (yes, obviously the title should have made that clear to me) while breaking up IRL. And of course Jen and Vince briefly got together while breaking up on-screen. Talk about a mind-fuck. He later said he couldn't deal with all the attention. I'm glad I'm not an artist and only have to go through emotional turmoil on one level.

My moment of realization was a scene at a concert. Or was supposed to be a scene at a concert. Although Brooke (Jen) and her live-in boyfriend, Gary (Vince), have already broken up, she invites him to a concert, thinking this will be a clear message that she wants them to give it another shot. (Even though, to be fair, she's also been bringing men over to the apartment to make him jealous.) They agree to meet there. He goes out drinking with his friends and doesn't show up, not at all realizing that this is supposed to be a definitive statement on their viability as a couple. But they're still sharing the apartment, so when she comes home and walks into her room after being stood up, she just can't take it and erupts into uncontrollable sobs. I knew it wasn't acting. Even when you're trying your absolute best to embody "conscious uncoupling" before Gwyneth gave it a name, it sucks.

It made me feel so much better. (Though somehow also worse.) Sometimes the thing that helps you get through hard moments is small, or embarrassing, or doesn't make sense at all. You might get a cat. You might dye your hair. You might then cut the hair you dyed. You might try the South Beach diet and realize you can spend your nights cutting up vegetables and trying not to think about how you're going to be cutting up "vegetables for one" while humming "I'll Be There for You" by the Rembrandts for the rest of your life. Sometimes you sit alone and cry after work after you've told everyone how "fine" you are. And despite your best coping mechanisms it can take months or years to get back out there. And that's OK.

I Was Wrong About John Mayer

Before I was born, my pop had taught himself to play the guitar. He was, and is, a very good guitar player, and I remember him playing "Yellow Submarine" when I was little. I know he could play lots of other songs, but that's the one I remember. Too bad, because the Beatles are pretty meh.

I wasn't crazy about them back then, either. Apparently two of my favorite songs when I was young were "Crocodile Rock" and "Benny and the Jets" by Elton John. My sister, Moosie, on the other hand, would stop crying if Steve Miller Band's "Abracadabra" came on the radio, and soon we'd see her little sausage fingers tapping along on her car seat.

My first concert was Aerosmith at what was then known as the Knickerbocker Arena in Albany. Four Non-Blondes opened. I loved the song "Dream On," and I remember Steven Tyler, his scarves swirling around his mic stand, whaling away and thinking about how the hot dog I was eating probably wasn't kosher. (I'm not kosher, but kosher hot dogs are the best.)

When I was studying for my AP history exam, I listened to that song, and that song alone, on repeat. When I got into the test, I was doing well and felt in the zone. Thoughts of Steven Tyler's strange but mesmerizing mouth did not cross my mind, which was, like an aspiring Supreme Court justice, entirely focused on the Constitution.

But then I got to the essay questions. The one I picked was on the Granger movement, and I went blank. Had I even heard of the Granger movement? I had. Hadn't I? I started to panic until suddenly "Dream On" popped into my head. I started humming along and went on to write what I recall being a brilliant essay on the Granger movement. I remember thinking Laura Ingalls Wilder would have been proud.

When I got my score back, it was a 5 out of 5. I was amazed. I always did well enough in school, but I was more like a B+/A- kind of girl. This was basically an A+!

I knew the music had something to do with it. I just did.

◆　◆　◆

Since then, I've associated particular music with different moods and moments in my life. When I'm on the train going upstate, I like Jackson Browne or Bonnie Raitt to get myself in the mood. When the sky is blue and the air is crisp, it's all Indigo Girls or Bruce Springsteen. When I need to drum up enthusiasm or motivation—especially cleaning out my closet—I go for "Caught Up in You" by 38 Special, "Africa" by Toto, or anything by Run DMC, Beastie Boys, or Florence and the Machine. And when I left the White House, crying like a baby in my car, I knew I needed fire, and I knew I needed to be able to paint the picture when I was ready to remember it. So I put on "Houses of the Holy" and then "Stairway to Heaven" as I drove out.

But my strongest music preference is well-known: jam bands. A lot of people don't get it, so let me try to explain. I started going to those concerts when I was around fourteen—my parents were hands-off—and got hooked. I loved the way improvisational music surprises you, and helps you forget where you are. My reward for good grades, cleaning my room, or just acting like a decent human—when I think about how I acted toward my mother as a teenager, it reaffirms my decision not to have kids—was an extra hour on my curfew when God Street Wine came to town. I spent most of the money I earned at my various jobs on concert tickets, and because they were always delivered by mail, there was no hiding them from my parents. Once my mom came into the house with two (equally sized) envelopes for me from the mailbox: a college rejection letter (Cornell, Brown, Georgetown...there were so many I lost track) and Phish tickets. That's me! The following summer, I saved up again and was lucky enough to see the Grateful Dead at the Knick before Jerry died.

In Rhinebeck, where I grew up, all the shows I went to were at the Rhinecliff Hotel. (To those in the know, it was simply "the Hotel.") Now it's a really posh boutique place that people from Manhattan stay in when they want to get away from it all, but back in 1991 it was a total dump, run by a misanthrope named Ed. Bands played in the back room, which featured exposed asbestos and rotting wood beams. You only drank things that came in containers with caps there. And even then you might want to wipe it off before you put your mouth on it. Everyone was always dripping with sweat, and the BO was beyond acknowledging. Going to these shows are some of the most joyful memories of my life.

Then I went away to college. Coming from a very small town, I had a hard time adjusting. The University of Vermont was downright bucolic, but my dorm had more kids than my high school graduating class. I was completely lonely, even though I made friends with some really nice women on my floor.

Things only started to turn around when God Street Wine came to Burlington. Though I was a Deadhead and Phish Phan, I was always a Wino at heart. The culture of GSW was truly welcoming—there was no litmus test. You didn't have to rattle off how many shows you'd been to or bring up obscure recordings you had. Everyone was there for the love of the music and the experience.

None of my new college friends had ever heard of them. So I did something I considered really courageous: I went to the show alone. I was super nervous and a little embarrassed. But as soon as I got there, those feelings went away. Everything was familiar. I felt at home.

That's how it's always been. No matter where I've lived, I could always find a show and meet people who got it. Sometimes I'd run into people I'd met at previous shows. When

GSW did their final show at the Wetlands in 1999, we didn't need to email each other. We knew we'd all be there.

After Jerry Garcia died in August of 1995, people mourned his life and talent and wondered what would happen to the music. The Dead has had several iterations over the years, and since the fall of 2015 has toured as Dead & Company with the original members Bob Weir, Bill Kreutzmann, and Mickey Hart, and new members Oteil Burbridge (formerly of the Allman Brothers and the Aquarium Rescue Unit), Jeff Chimenti (he once played backup for En Vogue!), and…John Mayer.

Yes, that John Mayer. "Your Body Is a Wonderland" John Mayer. John Mayer was taking on many of the Jerry leads.

I was very skeptical. John Mayer? The guy who did bad by Jennifer Aniston? How could that guy understand and attempt to approach the genius that was Jerry? He collects watches!

But he was spectacular. He respected the lyrics and the music and seemed humbled to tiptoe in Jerry's footsteps. I felt bad for doubting him.

I think Bobby and John summed up the mission of Dead & Company perfectly during an interview with Anthony Mason on *CBS Sunday Morning*, but what they said is also something broader we can all live by: It isn't about who's playing the music but about making sure the music goes on. Even learning that Ann Coulter was a Deadhead—shout-out to the *Slow Burn* podcast, which included this tidbit—did nothing to make me question my devotion. But it does make me question how much of a Deadhead Coulter really is.

Most-Played Songs on My iPhone as of 8/6/18

- "Catch My Breath"—Kelly Clarkson
- "Stairway to Heaven"—Led Zeppelin
- "Shut Up and Dance"—Walk the Moon
- "World on Fire"—Sarah McLachlan
- "Tried to Be True"—Indigo Girls
- "Heartbreaker"—Dionne Warwick
- "Gypsy"—Fleetwood Mac
- "Southern Cross"—Crosby, Stills, Nash & Young
- "Delilah"—Florence and the Machine
- "I Am Woman"—Helen Reddy
- "Howl"—Florence and the Machine
- "The Night They Drove Old Dixie Down"—The Band
- "Deal" (Live at Barton Hall, Cornell University 5/8/77)—The Grateful Dead
- "Can We Still Be Friends"—Mandy Moore
- "That's All"—Genesis
- "Smooth Criminal"—Michael Jackson
- "Somewhere"—Barbra Streisand
- "It's My Turn"—Diana Ross
- "There's No Place Like Home for the Holidays"—Perry Como (I must have had this sucker on repeat at Christmas)
- "Poison in the Well"—10,000 Maniacs

- "St. Stephen" (Dicks Picks, Fillmore Auditorium 11/8/69)—The Grateful Dead
- "Bridge Over Troubled Water" (Live, twenty-fifth anniversary Rock & Roll Hall of Fame Concert)—Simon and Garfunkel
- "Rock Me on the Water"—Jackson Browne
- "Wasted Time"—The Eagles

The Ones Who Got Away

I didn't date much in high school, college, or after. So I guess you could say I didn't date much at all. This can be chalked up to a number of factors, all of which are pretty boring. However, I did have some near misses that are, if not educational, entertaining:

1) THE FISHERMAN

When I lived in Boston and was working for John Kerry the first time, I met the Fisherman at a bar. He lived in Watertown and wore a hideous bracelet that I referred to as his Medic Alert. (Thus, his nickname among my friends: "Medic Alert Fisherman." We were very creative.) Nevertheless, I really liked him, and I programmed him into my phone—one of my first cell phones!—as "The Fisherman."

At work, one of my coworkers had a seven-year-old son

she'd bring to the office sometimes. Unlike the Fisherman, whose affections were not always clear, my coworker's son had a huge crush on me. He would always talk to me about my day, and about the incomprehensible things that seven-year-olds talk about.

He also liked to rifle through my purse and play with things in it, including my cell phone, which back then was a novelty to me as well as to any seven-year-olds who came across it. So naturally, one day, while his mom and I were in a meeting, he took out my cell phone and called the Fisherman twenty-seven times. I imagine the possibility of talking to a fisherman on the phone would be very exciting to a seven-year-old boy. Almost as good as an astronaut.

Today, slips of technology are understood, even de rigueur: All you have to say is "Sorry—butt-dial!" and everyone moves on. But back then this was how stalkers—or, rather, people who were too obsessed and became stalker-esque—operated. You called and hung up, called and hung up, either because you were too nervous to talk or because you were waiting for the other person to answer. The Fisherman thought I was calling until he answered.

As soon as I got out of the meeting and saw what the youngster had done, I called and apologized profusely. No answer, obviously. I didn't want to call him back again, because, well, yeah. But I left another message trying to explain what happened. He didn't call back. I got very nervous and tried again. But when he answered, all I got was "Nice try." Any hope I'd had of a nautical-themed summer sailed away.

2) DIABETIC-CAT GUY

Although my stint in Boston took place before I became a cat lady, I've always been a sucker for animals in need. So when a guy I was seeing mentioned his cat was diabetic, my heart panged, and I associated the strength of emotion with him.

This was around the holidays, and since I was in Boston and love the holidays, I wanted to do something Boston-appropriate. You only live once. I saved my money and bought two nosebleed seats to the Boston Pops and asked Diabetic-Cat Guy if he wanted to accompany me. He said yes.

I was really looking forward to it, but as the day approached I felt the telltale signs of a cold. By the day of, I was more snot than woman. But I didn't want to cancel—I didn't want to send DCG a bad signal, and I didn't want to miss the Boston Pops and lose the money I'd spent on the tickets.

So we went. And I was really not fun—not negative, exactly, but floppy and not talkative, and afterward I had nothing to say about this experience I'd told him repeatedly I was super excited about. We parted without kissing because I was so sniffly and weird.

The next day I emailed him to apologize for my vibe and to say I wish I'd been more fun. His reply, the last I would ever get from him, read: "It wouldn't have made a difference."

3) THE SET-UP

When I first moved to DC, my friend Sean set me up with someone he knew I'd hit it off with. Setting people up: Why does no one do it anymore? It really works! I mean, in this particular instance it didn't work, but it definitely could have. Being set up helps you avoid going into dates with preconceived notions about whether someone is going to be "compatible" with you. Sometimes your friends know you better than you know yourself. Even though you can essentially accomplish the same thing with Hinge, one of the Tinder spin-offs that uses mutual Facebook friends to pair you off with someone, I don't think that's the same, because it allows you to Google-stalk before, eliminating the opportunity for a leap of faith. You could, of course, abstain from Google-stalking before the date, on principle, but who has that kind of willpower?

I immediately liked the Set-Up a lot. A lot a lot. He was extremely handsome and fun, and he took me to a bar called Gazuza, which was funny. Even though I wasn't in the habit of sleeping with people on the first date per se, I would have.

But he never made a move. And then we went out to dinner, and he never made a move. And then we went to lunch, and lunch again, and he never made a move. I know, I know—why didn't *I* make a move? Because I didn't! Don't be like me! By the time he disappeared we had never kissed. It was a bummer.

Fast-forward six years: I'm sitting in my apartment in

DC watching *Barefoot Contessa* while I make myself breakfast before work on a Saturday. Sometimes she takes video questions, and as I was tending to my muesli I heard a familiar voice. "Hi, Ina, I'm [the Set-Up]. I'm preparing a party for my boyfriend and…"

Maybe some people would consider this dodging a bullet. A guy who calls Ina Garten to help with his boyfriend's party? Can't he handle it himself? I, however, am not one of those people. I love Ina Garten. Don't get me wrong— I'm happy about how things worked out. (Hi, DK!!!) But I maintain we would have been a great match.

4) DIET CRUSH

I didn't really hook up in college. Then, at the end of my senior year at Wisconsin, I met a guy at a bar. Maybe it was the alcohol, or the fact that I was on the brink of a new and exciting post-graduation life, but for some reason I thought I'd finally cracked the code: I was going to get a boyfriend. I had no plans for a job yet, so the logistics of falling in love didn't faze me. I'm go-with-the-flow anyway. You figure it out. Especially if the guy is as handsome as he was.

I took him home, and he slept over. After the stuff, he looked up at my bureau and noticed I had a framed photo. "How do you know Kim Endsley?" he asked incredulously. They went to nursery school together. This was just one more indication that we were destined to become a couple. I knew someone he went to nursery school with!

Then, the next morning as he was getting dressed he happened to look under the bed.

"Why do you have a case of Diet Crush under your bed?" he asked.

"Because I love it?" I replied.

It turns out he had a girlfriend.

5) THE COLLECTOR

My friends and I were meeting up with a group of people at a bar in Union Square. I was twenty-three. Everyone was playing pool when someone called me over. "This guy went to Madison, too," they said. Although he was wearing pleated khakis and a short-sleeve button-down, my political radar wasn't as sensitive as it was after working in DC for a couple of years, so I didn't immediately register him as conservative. He introduced himself. I won't say what his actual name was, so let's call him "Rocky Bay." It was that level of amusing and that kind of vibe. Nevertheless, he was kind of cute.

As I always did when I went out, I introduced myself as Paloma. Although it was New York, we went to the same bars all the time, and the scene, as much as there was one, still felt small. Everyone I knew lived in Manhattan with about two too many roommates. You couldn't get a taxi to take you to Brooklyn late into the 2000s, and it didn't occur to many people, myself included, that the living situation would be more pleasant (like, one person per bedroom) there. Everyone was also a little more paranoid when you couldn't confirm strangers' identities on your phone during a quick trip to the bathroom.

We didn't chat for very long before he asked me if I wanted to go back to his apartment and hang out. For someone who had never been bought a drink in a bar before, this felt somewhat momentous, even from a guy in pleated khakis named Rocky Bay. I didn't stop to think about how weird it was that he was asking me out after so little small talk, so I agreed.

We took a cab to his place on the west side. Glamorous. We made small talk about some of our favorite places in Madison. He didn't seem to have the same love for the Plaza, a wonderful/terrible bar, that I did; I guess he didn't like having to think about whether he'd need a tetanus shot after leaning against a bar on a night out. But that was half the fun!

In retrospect this should have been my first sign. Who doesn't love the Plaza?

His apartment was a small one-bedroom. I was impressed initially, but within a minute of walking in, I felt the presence of something strange. Something eerie. Something like hundreds of Beanie Babies in his bedroom.

No, not something "like" hundreds of Beanie Babies in his bedroom. There were hundreds of Beanie Babies in this guy's bedroom. Shelves dedicated to Beanie Babies lined the walls; floppy cats and thematic bears drooped off the dresser. I'd always thought they were cute. I wondered if he, like so many other Beanie Babies collectors in the '90s, assumed they would appreciate in value and make him rich one day.

I'd not had many one-night stands before, but I was fairly certain this was not normal. And I don't know if any amount of casual sex could prepare a person for this. I didn't know what to say, or do, so I ended up staying for about two hours, thanking God I'd told him my name was Paloma. Eventually, because I'd had a couple of drinks, I figured out how to use that as an excuse to leave. As we were saying "Let's get together again soon," I was certain I'd never see him again. Since he lived on the west side and there weren't many ATMs back then, I didn't have money for a cab, so I used my remaining $1.50 to buy an apple juice for my long walk home.

I assumed that was that. While I didn't mention the Beanie Babies explicitly, I thought the bewildered look on my face when I saw them communicated my disinterest. I mean, there were *a lot* of Beanie Babies. If I'd been more cynical back then I might have wondered if they had drugs in them.

But then he called and asked me out on a date. And by "asked me out on a date," I mean left a voice mail on the machine I shared in the one-bedroom with Cara, Volpe, and Okas.

At first I was excited: I never got asked out on dates! Once again, I felt like I had cracked a code. I was reaching a milestone. My life was progressing.

But then he suggested the place.

Of course an adult man who collects Beanie Babies is not

going to have the most sophisticated taste in restaurants. But all my friends, when they got asked out, went to semi-cool places. Not expensive, but the kind of things you read about in magazines. At the time it was "fusion" cuisine. Some amount of neurotic effort—maybe a lot—went into the suggestion of where to go. Looking back, I feel almost nauseated thinking about what low self-esteem I must have had to agree to this. But I assumed that my friends were so much prettier and more interesting than I was, and I should take what I could get. So when Rocky Bay, Beanie Babies collector, said he would meet me at the Señor Frog's in Washington Square, I was, once again, made speechless by him.

And then I agreed to go. At some point I must have told him my name wasn't really Paloma.

A Note on Sex

I don't have much to say about it.

Altared States

By the time I started thinking about what it would be like to be married, America was in the throes of *Sex and the City* mania. While some of the quotes and story lines are timeless—the baby shower! Big! The reveals of a new lover's unusual sexual proclivity!—much of it is dated. We could dissect the problematic implications of Carrie's comments on bisexuality for pages, but I'll leave that to the professionals. At the time, viewers like me were mainly engaged in a rigorous project of comparison and personality diagnosis, by which I mean: Was I a Charlotte, Miranda, Carrie, or Samantha?

Definitely not a Samantha (I appreciate promiscuity in others but never was a natural at it myself) or a Charlotte (not so uptight). Probably a mix of Carrie and Miranda. I was not as chic as Carrie (but I like to think I have flair!) or as reasonable as Miranda. Organized, but not pragmatic. That said, they both had suspicions about marriage. And like them, I really can't say I thought much about getting married growing up. I didn't conscript neighborhood boys into "marrying" me in staged weddings or dream about my dress. My parents eloped! My friends never really talked about it—we talked about music or parties or school—and because I didn't date much, my brain was on a different track. (I guess if you don't date much you—wisely—spend your time doing things besides planning your future wedding.) Throughout high school, college, and my twenties, the only person I ever imagined marrying was Matthew McConaughey circa *A Time to Kill* and *Contact*. Maybe this was a defense mechanism to keep me from having to worry about how I felt about establishing an ideally permanent bond to another person. While I genuinely think Matthew would find me charming—I was just keeping livin', like his foundation says!—I don't think I was ever in any danger of having to choose between marrying him and sticking with the single lifestyle that had been serving me so well.

The thought honestly didn't cross my mind in any meaningful way until the moment DK—whose given name is David and who is, as I've mentioned, definitely my husband—proposed to me. I was flabbergasted and panicked!

Before I go on to reveal my soft underbelly here, I need to clearly state up front that none of my panic or how I felt had anything to do with DK himself.

We dated routinely. There was no drama of the "Will he call?!?!" variety. After our very DC courtship we agreed that until something changed we would go out on Wednesdays and Saturdays. Easy to plan and execute for our busy schedules. We went on two trips before we got married, one to Turks and Caicos and then one to Utah after we had gotten engaged around my birthday. While most people test compatibility on trips like this, we were too tired from working in the White House (me) and in the Senate (DK) to use our crankiness with each other as a reliable indicator of our long-term prospects. We slept a lot. And I had my share of prickly pear margaritas.

DK and I had talked a few times about the idea of getting married before he proposed. (I think this is what most couples do now—right? It's more than a little retro to spring it on the woman completely unawares. And the idea of DK nervously approaching my dad for his "blessing" before asking me is hilarious.) I was thirty-seven and already knew I had mega fertility issues, so it wasn't like the clock was ticking, but I began to feel very…curious. It was kind of like how you never wear orange because you just know deep down that orange won't look good on you—whenever anyone asks if you ever wear orange, you assure them that there's nothing *wrong* with wearing orange, you like it on other people, but it's just not for you—but then one day someone is like, "Why not try on this orange dress?" and you find it really works with your skin tone. Except this isn't the best analogy because marriage would be like wearing the orange dress every day for the rest of your life. Was that something that could happen to me?

Instead of treating this as a new and exciting experience to think about and explore, following the engagement (which was almost as shocking as the terrifying size of the ring), I really started to feel, and act, like a spoiled teenager with "emotional problems."

I still had my apartment on M Street, which was expensive even without taking into account my government salary. But I could walk to the White House, so I'd always considered it worth it, and part of me was also proud to be able to pay for it on my own. I'd signed the lease from Chicago, sight unseen, right after we won the 2008 election, and although I was rolling the dice about what would fit or work by ordering everything from Crate & Barrel in Chicago instead of waiting until I got to DC—I was excited!—the day I picked out my couch and end tables was one of the most fun of my life. My friend Anne had to help me get up the nerve to make such large purchases by pre-gaming our shopping trip with champagne. The furniture wasn't just nice; it felt like freedom—it was the first time I had picked out what I really wanted and not just taken what was at Salvation Army or on sale at Target. And getting rid of it felt like the exact opposite.

I also couldn't help but think: *If I move out of my apartment and give away my furniture and he changes his mind, I will never be able to afford this nice Crate & Barrel furniture ever again.*

It's a googlable fact that DK has what you might call "means." He hadn't been a humble government employee his whole life, only for about five years at that point, and he had a real savings account, investments, and a town house in Georgetown. Whereas some people might have felt safe and secure marrying a man with some financial stability, I thought it had to be some kind of trap. I became obsessed with figuring out how I could ever "contribute"—the word I used—in a meaningful way. I started mentally tallying all my positive attributes—funny, encyclopedic knowledge of *Friends*, uh…good at planning vacations…—trying to determine whether they equaled DK's financial assets.

This added another dimension to my paranoia: It was not just about my potential loss of Crate & Barrel furniture, but about what my attachment to that furniture represented about what I perceived to be the imbalance of the relationship. I mean, Crate & Barrel is nice, but it's not that nice. I reasoned it was only a matter of time before DK realized I was not fancy. (If it took him more than ten seconds around me to have this realization, that would have been an *actual* problem.) Having worked on campaigns and in government nearly my whole adult life, I lived by the idea that things always come to an end, sometimes when you don't expect it.

Plus, *Sex and the City* was haunting me. As a Carrie Bradshaw disciple, I know few scenes of any movie or TV show better than (1) when Carrie and Aidan break up and she sits on the floor in her bathroom for four hours because she just couldn't agree to marry him, and (2) when she finally does agree to get married, she gets left at the fucking altar!

So instead of starting an adult conversation about my anxieties, I would casually leave the *Sex and the City* movie on and pause it at the part where Big jumps out of the car and Carrie says, "I KNEW YOU WOULD DO THIS" and those beautiful roses are weaponized. At which point I would mutter, "Isn't that *terrible?*" in order to convey to

DK that he'd better not be thinking about doing any such thing. I would not even have the consolation of a fabulous blue bird headpiece.

So anyway. All this was just swirling around in my head because I had been sleeping at DK's most nights anyway; the understanding was that when my lease was up I just wouldn't renew it. I think. We'd been engaged about six months when I got my lease renewal in my mailbox. If he hadn't changed his mind in six months, maybe we were all good?

Carrie Bradshaw strikes again.

Nothing ever made me feel better than when Carrie went to the bank to get a loan, and at age thirty-five, she only had $800 in savings. At the same age I had about $1,800. I was incredibly responsible!

Not that responsible. Instead of leaving the apartment, I stealthily went month to month for six more months. In the meantime, I stewed and picked fights about dumb stuff. Trying to nudge and prod any bad behavior that I possibly could to see if it would make him flee. Shrummie was giving me the face like, *Don't blow up our spot, lady! I'm not going back to M Street!*

Finally, one night after work I was grumbling on the couch about whether there would ever be wall space for my "artwork." DK asked, "Is something wrong?"

I was like a startled animal—suddenly my voice was squeaky and I was choking back tears. I spilled my guts— I described my angst about money (and not really having any), how it freaked me out because I didn't know what bills I should or *could* pay, how I had no idea what I actually brought to the relationship besides my then-fourteen-pound cat. (Since I got him, he went on a diet.) And most importantly—and most scarily—what I would do if it didn't work out and I had given up all my worldly possessions. I relayed my many concerns over where my "art" would go. I had collected a lot of knickknacks and street art on my travels with POTUS, and I assumed DK would think it was tacky and forbid me from putting on the walls of "his" tastefully decorated three-thousand-square-foot home. I was about to enter the realm of extreme privilege, "uptown problems," which created another neurosis: Who was I to be complaining about any of this, really?

By this point you probably know enough about me to think this seems out of character. I am not usually so neurotic, and I've come close to shitting my pants in front of famous people too many times to be particularly concerned with what other people think. Or maybe you're doing an *Us Weekly* and thinking, *Senior White House staff—they're just like us!* I have to assume I was freaking out so much because I really cared. The amount of panicked text messages you send to your girlfriends about a problem—even a made-up problem—is usually a good measure of your investment in something.

I should have brought it all up sooner, because I would have saved myself a lot of time and energy. That's the big lesson here. At the end of this weird, sad, and cathartic con-versation, DK said, "Well, OK, if you ever think you might want to get divorced someday, I will move to a hotel."

DK is the best.

Oh, OK. That was it. We didn't have insurmountable problems. We didn't have problems at all. I had issues with money, asymmetry, and space, and since DK doesn't have issues with those things at all, he could have easily made me feel better if I'd just brought it up sooner instead of spinning myself a web of fixations. I am incredibly lucky that this is the only problem I had to deal with before getting married, and that it was so easily solved.

That was about six years ago, and neither of us has, to my knowledge, wanted to get divorced yet. Except for the time DK agreed to move to Williamsburg so that I could be close to work while our condo was under construction. We thought it would only last a few weeks in that apartment, which was equipped with what was alleged to be a queen bed—which, even for two short people, is not sufficient—and two white pleather love seats. (When Shrummie tried to jump on them, he'd slide backward and fall off.) The building was full of recent college grads who would do all the things recent college grads do. We ended up living there for nine months. It wasn't 100 percent clear we were going to make it.

But we did. And I guess the biggest lesson I've learned from marriage, which is not something I ever thought I'd say, is that we all have our shit. We tell ourselves we're crazy, which then makes talking about what's upsetting us seem shameful. It isn't. Anything that's bothering you matters. But you shouldn't torture the other person—who could quite possibly be an innocent bystander to your personal anxieties—by not saying anything about it.

And for what it's worth, our house is now full of my crazy patterned quilted shit and DK loves it! Or says he loves it. Maybe "tolerates it" is a better way to put it. And I appreciate it! The other night when I was working on this book, I needed to clear my head, so I went into the bedroom to watch the final season of *House of Cards*, Petey the cat by my side. I woke up the next morning to find DK asleep on the couch. When I asked why he didn't come to bed, he said he didn't want to disturb me (or Petey). It may seem small, but the small things are what comprise a life together.

What's on My Nightstand

- *Hello!* UK. I have a subscription because I love the royals and find them soothing.
- Mountain Ocean Skin Trip moisturizer: It's awesome and reminds me of being in high school.
- Books I haven't read.
- Picture of me and my Omie.
- Headphones so I can listen to my nightly BBC Global podcast and not disturb DK.
- Bobby pins: I have to pin my bangs back when I go to sleep so I don't get zits on my forehead. Writing these lists, I'm realizing how much of my daily routine centers around avoiding zits.
- An extra pair of cheap glasses: I like to watch my beloved Ina Garten to calm my soul before I go to sleep. However, when I do fall asleep, I don't want to crush my good glasses.

What to Expect When You're Not Expecting

I have to be honest: A woman discussing her decision (if it's a decision) not to have kids is always so fraught and complicated that I didn't really want to write about it. Although things are changing, the pressures are still there: You always have to justify yourself. You need a clear *reason*. Even if it's just "I really didn't want them! The prospect of changing a diaper is repulsive to me!" (And even that inspires people who have changed diapers to assure you that you're wrong: It's different when they're *your* baby's diapers.) You're expected to know exactly why you're forty-two years old and never put your uterus to use-r-us. There's not a lot of room for uncertainty. Probably because biology doesn't leave much room for uncertainty: The clock keeps ticking. And periods! Monthly, often painful reminders that your body can grow a human. That growing a human is technically what it's for.

I wrote a little bit about not having kids in my first book: about how, on my thirty-fifth birthday, I walked into the

Navy Mess, and Reggie Love greeted me with something like, "MASTRO! According to CNN, you are officially of 'advanced maternal age'!" (And I established in the first book that Reggie is one of the most intellectually curious and kind people I know—he wasn't trying to hurt my feelings, but really just sharing knowledge.) At which point I thought, *Fair enough. I wonder if I'm still fertile.* I persuaded my beloved gyno to give me an AMH test, which measures the quantity (not quality!) of eggs you're working with. He didn't want to do it; they only like to do this test if you are actively "trying." I really don't know why I felt like I needed it, but I persisted until he gave in. The range is from 0 to 7, and I was something like a 0.2.

I think I wrote about it at the time mainly to answer the question that's always in the back of people's minds when they meet a woman of advanced—or post—maternal age with no offspring to show for it: Why? I can get annoyed with people asking, especially if it's totally out of context, and especially if I remember that no one really cares if men stay childless bachelors playing video games in their underwear for their entire lives, but I also think it's understandable that people want to know. Even though things are changing, having kids is still the default. Now that the word is out there about why I don't, people ask me less. Though being asked is preferable to people assuming that I must have them, which then makes me irate and requires me to go into awkward detail about why I don't, to demonstrate how rude I find the assumption.

Still, I didn't really examine my feelings about not having

kids at length, except to say that I wasn't particularly sad about it and that I was kind of happy to have the decision taken away from me. I didn't get into how other people treat you when you're a woman who doesn't have kids, or what not having them, in this culture and in this world right now, means for how you come to see the second half of your life. Which you also can't really believe you're in.

So when I decided that I needed to write about it again, I stared at the computer screen for way too long. Did I want to tell an encouragingly cheerful "Your body, your choice!" kind of story? Or was I more a resolute, powerful "Don't feel sorry for me: I'm not a cautionary tale" kind of story?

Both of those things are true. But what I actually want to do is tell a new kind of story.

◆ ◆ ◆

When I was in middle school, I was obsessed with names. I think mostly because nobody had my name. (Yes, in 1976 "Alyssa" belonged to me and then-four-year-old Alyssa Milano.) My mom told me that I was named after one of her favorite campers she met when she was a camp counselor. When I asked her what that Alyssa was like, my mom said she was fun, easy to be around, and a very can-do girl— which is basically what I felt I was. I became obsessed with making sure my future kids would have names that set them up to become the life of the party, successful, and rich. Any time I encountered a name that seemed up to this task, I would write it down in a notebook I had for this purpose.

By high school, I remember the names that topped the list were Persephone, Marley, and Eden. The latter two were characters on soap operas (Marley: *Another World*; Eden: *Santa Barbara*), and I thought they both seemed like nice people. When I learned Persephone was the Greek goddess who ruled the underworld with her husband, Hades, I balked, but then I reasoned that maybe this is exactly the kind of person who would become both the life of the party and rich.

Since I never had many boyfriends in high school or college, I never dreamed of having a wedding. I would get whiffs of sadness about not being asked out when I saw my friends having fun with guys, but I was never that envious once I saw them in the throes of the "Will he call?!?!?!" drama. (Which, unfortunately, continues for about as long as acne does: way longer than you think.) But I did always think about having kids. What do I mean by "think about"? I don't mean fantasized about, necessarily, or yearned for them. It's just that when I envisioned my future, I put kids in there.

I graduated and had a fun life, full of surprises and twists and turns and things I couldn't have done if I had been too worried about locking down any one aspect of my existence, including kids. I moved to New York City, then Boston, then DC. That's when I felt like I was fully living my dream: I was working for John Kerry. What more could I possibly want than to sit at the front desk and answer phones for $20,500? I'm not even joking!

That's also when I met Doug. He (1) never wanted to

get married and (2) never wanted to have kids. He was very clear about this. I didn't care about the first issue; the second issue seemed so far in the future for me as to be irrelevant. In what felt like no time at all, after all the months of waiting around for a job in politics, all the rejections I'd gotten, I'd gone from being ecstatic at the opportunity to work as a lowly general assistant to being a senior member of Kerry's team.

Doug and I both worked on the presidential campaigns, and life was crazy. I can't tell whether campaigns were better or worse before social media and the internet; the Obama campaign was intense—and LONG—but the Kerry campaign felt so much more draining. We were like a dysfunctional family that really wants to throw the perfect reunion but can't pull it off. I couldn't think about anything besides what was directly in front of me.

Then, all of a sudden, when I thought I was going to have to sign up for unemployment because JK had lost the election and we weren't going to the White House, Barack Obama called.

This is going to sound basic, but our thoughts and feelings don't come from just one source. There are many reasons we feel what we feel and think what we think. Timing is a big one. The people we have around us is another. I was never not present at work those days. I continued to feel like I was living my dream, and like I couldn't let down Barack Obama, whom I so admired and respected. He—and my other bosses—believed in me and were giving me a shot. I didn't want to blow it. You could say my work was my life, but I wasn't thinking of it in those terms. It was more that what I wanted to be doing with my life and my life were aligned. Even when my gums were bleeding from stress. I never thought my dream life would be easy or without problems.

Despite the high stakes, the Obama crew all had a lot of fun. I know it sounds cheesy, but I'm not trying to be metaphorical—I felt, deep down, that these people were a kind of family to me. I mean, we spent more time together, and endured more stressful situations, than I ever have with my actual family. (Whom I also love—hi, Mummy!) From the time we all moved out to Chicago to launch the Obama campaign in February 2007 until I left the White House in May 2014, I always felt like I had a family. And the family dynamic had me in the roles of jolly matriarch if I was the boss or rascally—yet wise—little sister if we're talking about the bros in the White House.

When I was director of scheduling and advance, most of the team were a few years younger than I was, or more, and they always called me "AM" or "Mama." I started referring to them as "the kids." I don't know why I seem sage—I'm a five-foot-two goofball who frequently plays air guitar to the Grateful Dead in the office—but the kids knew that if you came to AM for advice, you should be prepared for real talk. And they came often.

I helped them get better credit for their work, badgered them to wear more "structured" clothing to the office, deciphered what emails from their crushes might mean, and told them when it was time to fly the coop and when they weren't quite ready for the next step. I gave blessings on plans for wedding proposals and would not be shy about saying "I see the way she looks at babies, but you are too young to have kids—enjoy being married for a bit!"

One of my favorite memories was when Rahm Emanuel, who was the White House chief of staff at the time, decided to leave to run for mayor of Chicago. He called me to his office and said, "Honey, I'm gonna do this. I need the best. Who do you have for me?" (Please don't draw any #Metoo suspicion in Rahm calling me "honey"—he even called Axelrod "honey.")

He meant he wanted to snag people from our staff and take them with him. And I knew immediately who should go. Like a tiny Liam Neeson, circa *Taken*, in a J.Crew skirt suit, I called (Mike) Faulman and (Michael) Ruemmler down into my office on the ground floor of the West Wing and said, "Listen, guys: You are going to leave me." I told them all the reasons why they should go. I told them that sometimes you have to leave to come back, and that sometimes you have to have new experiences to get to the next level. Within two weeks they had both moved to Chicago. And though it sucked to say goodbye, we all agreed it was the right thing to do. I'm not joking when I say that one of my biggest accomplishments in the White House was building a team that could last beyond the eighteen acres. And they did just as much for me. Not to mention all the people who talked me down from various IBS panic attacks.

OK, you're thinking. *That's really sweet. But that's at work. What about when you're at home? Weren't you lonely? Who did*

you have when you needed to unwind with reality TV and a goblet
of wine?

When November 2007 rolled around, I had to face the facts that with the Iowa caucuses on the horizon, I would not, for the first time ever, be able to go home to Rhinebeck for Thanksgiving. This was hard for me to admit—not as hard as missing Christmas would have been, but I love the holidays and I love my mom and pop and all our German traditions.[1] And the weather in Chicago was getting more Chicago-y every day.

I called Mom and Pop to tell them the news. I expected a lecture or at least some moderate sadness. Instead I got excitement. "What if we came to you?!"

Why didn't I think of that? Well, because I couldn't think of very much. By the week of, like many of my colleagues, I had no time to cook or think about what I might have cooked if I'd had time to cook. But being someone who works well under pressure, I shifted into plan-B mode: We were all going to have a proper Thanksgiving with the family we had. I ordered some prepared Thanksgiving

---

1   My mom's family is from Alsace and Bavaria, which means I have cravings for dampfnudeln, Pfannkuchen (with blueberries), Käsespätzle, Apfelstrudel (nearly impossible to find one like Omie used to make—I think it's the Austrian recipe, which has a bit of sour cream in it), and Zwetschgenkuchen. My mom also makes the best Rouladen.
   The other half of my family is from Italy—hence Mastromonaco—and my dad's family comes from Castellino del Biferno in the province of Campobasso. Pop makes zeppole every Christmas morning—I like mine with tupelo honey—and I also love arancini (rice balls), ricotta cookies (I make these every Christmas), red sauce, and obviously meatballs. Like many people with IBS, I love a digestif, so limoncello, or an espresso with sambuca and a lemon twist, always hits the spot.

staples from a store called Fox & Obel. Emmett, my director of advance, whose wife, Catherine, was traveling to Chicago so they could celebrate their first Thanksgiving as a married couple, pitched in.

The day of was weird and windy, but Emmett and I acted like siblings on a mission. We went to pick up our order and began zooming around the aisles grabbing what we didn't have and anything else that looked good. It wasn't going to be perfect, but it was going to be something.

Mom, Pop, and Moosie came. I was living with Smoot at the time, and her boyfriend—now husband—was there, too. Dey showed up and taught my mom what a mimosa was, and then sat with her enjoying a few. Pop made apple pie, Smoot's boyfriend did a key lime, and Shrum contributed by repeatedly jumping on the counter. By dessert, Doug (by then a beloved ex); my friend Devorah; Reggie; and Gibbs; his wife, Mary Catherine; and their son, Ethan, were all there. Ethan loved the L train that ran right below our apartment and spent a long time watching it go by with Shrum.

And then a year later we won the election.

I always felt wildly lucky.

◆ ◆ ◆

But it wasn't as if I didn't notice I was getting older—even if I didn't see the changes in my face and body, or note the passing of each birthday, people love to comment on it. Even well-meaning people. When Doug and I broke up in 2005, I was twenty-nine. In those days, and in DC especially, twenty-nine was not the twenty-nine it is now. Turning thirty was much more of a thing. People thought you should get married and have kids even if you were obviously too busy, too broke, and too single to be thinking about it. *Sex and the City* broke barriers, definitely, but everyone also understood those women as characters on TV. Larger than life. Different from life. I paid nervous attention to all the new talk about how women, focused on moving up in their careers, were now waiting too long to have kids. I wondered if that was going to happen to me. But it wasn't something I lost sleep over. I didn't have anyone to have a kid with, and I didn't have the money or time or strong enough desire to be a single mother. I guess you could say I was choosing to put my career ahead of having a family, but I really wasn't thinking in those terms. I felt like I had made choices throughout my twenties in order to get to the career I wanted, at which point I was just living my life.

And then Reggie forced me to reckon with it. Once he said the phrase, the blaring factoid kept flashing bright in my brain: *advanced maternal age!*

I got the news about my (lack of) fertility just after I'd landed from a trip to Afghanistan and was at a party at the Italian or French embassy—can't remember—for the Elle Women in DC annual soiree.

I stepped outside, took the call, and went back to the party.

I can't say I wasn't rattled—it was strange to get a call saying that there was basically nothing going on in my womb and nothing ever going to go on down there. All those horrible period cramps and painful chin zits for 0.2?

Still, I didn't feel the world coming to an end. I was very fulfilled. I had just gone to Afghanistan and was at a party at the French or Italian embassy. The next year I'd go to Paris Fashion Week and meet Kanye West. (When I told him I worked for Barack Obama, he said, "Cool.") That was that. My life was going to go on, just without a kid in it.

◆   ◆   ◆

Today, I mostly feel the same way: I think not having a kid is right for me. I don't ever have to stay in a job I hate and can take big risks without worrying about how they'll impact my family. I can still travel a lot, on short notice, and my indecision about whether I'll ever go back into politics affects no one but me (and DK, and the cats, both of whom can handle themselves) and the people I talk to about it. It would be much harder for me to pick up work on another campaign if I had a toddler running around.

I can't imagine being pregnant anyway. My lifelong stomach problems make the idea of messing around anywhere near that area simply not appealing. In any way whatsoever. I'm not going to go into detail about it, but the things you hear about what happens during pregnancy…well, they seem like they would be exponentially worse with IBS. When I've said that to other people, they don't understand, but most people don't understand what it feels like to constantly worry your gut might blow open because you were craving an omelet. I'm sure there are lots of graphic blog posts about dealing with IBS and pregnancy, but I'm never going to go through it, so I'm not going to go there. Godspeed to anyone who does. I also never considered IVF, or a surrogate, or any of the new technologies that have allowed people who really want a child to have one. Besides the whole pregnancy thing, that stuff—IVF—never really interested me. It seemed like so much work, and I already had so much work. And also disappointment. People who know me know I really don't manage disappointment well. Which I have to assume means I don't really, really want to have a kid.

But. But! This is the thing everyone wants to know: Am I *sure*?

Well, no. And I don't know why.

The most unexpected side effect of leaving the White House in 2014 was the sudden sense that I was no longer needed. I had withdrawal from not seeing the WH family every day, for sure, but although I'd expected to feel carefree, light, and enthusiastic about waking up after 8:00 AM, I just felt unimportant. What was the point of me anymore? It was what I imagine empty-nest syndrome feels like.

So of course that made me think that I (we) should maybe have kids. Though I can't physically have one (barring divine intervention), we could always adopt. After the White House, I also had a lot of time on my hands, trying to figure out what to do next, and having a kid would definitely have been something to do.

There was also a growing sense that, if I wanted to be

truly successful, I needed to have a kid. If you think of life as like a video game, I beat "career," and now kids are the next level. I'm a successful person who wants to do things better than everyone else does them. Not in a competitive-with-other-people way—I'm competitive with myself. And our society tells you that "having it all" as a woman, despite being widely acknowledged as impossible, means happily balancing career and kids. There's an idea that motherhood is what makes you into your complete self as a woman.

There are also other pressures. When I make plans with friends who have kids, I feel like my schedule suddenly loses all meaning. Though I think I convince myself of this more than anyone actually puts it on me, if I have a conflict on the one day a week that a mother has free, I move my appointments around, and I do it happily. I feel like I should always qualify any complaint about how busy I am with something like, "I know my problems are nothing compared to how hard you"—subtext: a mother—"must work." And it's not wrong, necessarily.

I wonder, too, if people ask me to do work for them so often because they know I don't have kids. When I would tell people I couldn't do a speech or attend an event because I was working on this book, for example, I got a sort of eye-rolling pushback. But I know that if I said, "Sorry, I can't participate on the panel this week because my daughter has piano lessons and then we're doing a family dinner," I would be met with resounding understanding and "Say no more!" On the weekends I feel like a very chill pariah: DK plays golf many weekends, but I have very few friends to hang out with because weekends are designated "family time" for people with kids. I wouldn't even broach the topic of a cheeky Saturday afternoon cocktail or Friday night movie with someone with kids. This makes me feel frivolous: At forty-two, should I really be hanging out and smoking pot all weekend? Shouldn't I be doing more "adult" activities? (I also literally bake!) I understand this is a ridiculous thing to worry about—precisely because I'm an adult (who works hard), I shouldn't be worrying about whether I'm filling my time appropriately. I've earned whatever pockets of peace I can find.

The bigger anxiety, though, is that I'm a second-tier person in people's lives. And it's not totally projecting. This is a reality, not a complaint. I'm not *not* a second-tier person in people's lives. I would hope your kids are first tier!

Of course, I know all this isn't what's really important in the decision. You don't need to be a mother to be a "complete" woman. (There's no such thing.) Life is not a video game. Feeling unneeded is not a good reason to have a baby. Wanting something to do is not a good reason to have a baby. A baby is not a "project"—a baby is a human. I don't feel deeply maternal (though I execute being maternal at a high level), and I don't have a strong yearning to see a little version of myself, complete with IBS, running around. When I see a really cute baby, or I've been picking out a gift for my third baby shower in as many weeks, I can get bummed. But all I need to cure that feeling is to see a troupe of snotty six-year-olds Razor-scooter toward me on the sidewalk and I feel better.

(Disclaimer for the moms out there: I know you love your kids. I'm not saying you don't. But I also know you hate the Razor scooters, too.)

As I've been writing this, I've worried that any of my kid-negative comments—"snotty" is a telltale anti-kid word, but they literally are! You don't learn to control your own snot until at least age fourteen for girls, and much later for boys!—will incite outrage among mothers. How dare I criticize their choice? It's as if you can't talk about what's right for you, what your feelings are, without implying that every other woman should share them. (I notice that men don't have this problem.)

On the flip side, there are the people—never actual friends, but people I barely know—who sit me down and say, in their most seriously sympathetic voice, "Alyssa, it's not too late." I know they mean well—they just want me to be as happy as they are. But the most important consideration in having a kid is whether it's right for *you* specifically, not some random woman you meet at a conference. I am also very aware that I have "options." How could I get so far in my life and career and not understand that I have "options" if I want to have a child? The idea that I'll one day wake up and regret not having a kid suggests both that I don't know myself and that having a child is a rite of passage that everyone should experience. If I do wake up and regret it, it's not really anyone else's business. One time someone invited me to a fund-raiser for Hillary Clinton, and I showed up only to find that it was a mother-daughter event. Despite my conviction that being child-free doesn't make me less of a woman or person, I felt totally humiliated, like everyone was simultaneously pitying me (because what kind of sad person goes to a mother-daughter event without bringing a mother or a daughter?) and judging me. I didn't even have a female cat at the time. And I don't think I felt so ashamed because I was desperate, deep down, to have a daughter of my own.

Or am I? This is the struggle for me. The question isn't resolved. Having a kid is making a decision and setting a clear path: kid, for eighteen years, plus all the shit they do in college that you have to bail them out of. That's your main priority, or at least one of your main priorities. When you don't have one, the path could go in many more directions. Including what some might consider the excessive acquisition of rescue cats. And including, actually, eventually having a kid. I never want to say, flat out, that I don't want one, because these cultural and social pressures make it so difficult to determine what you actually feel. If I wake up one day and feel like I need to adopt something bigger than a large Persian cat, is it because I actually want to, or is it because I watched my sister, my bestie from Copake, and my veterinary neurosurgeon/Godsend all have children this year, and, yeah, I'll be honest, I felt kind of bad? Not betrayed, but left out, or missing out, and somehow abandoned.

I still lean toward no. I think that if I really wanted one, I'd know it—that all this wavering and analyzing wouldn't matter, because my desire to have a kid would supersede any sense of the downsides. I'm a huge champion of gut feelings, and mine have never led me astray before. So why is this the only thing I can't be 100 percent sure about? On the one hand, it's amazing that at forty-two, I can be so unsure of where the rest of my life is going. In the past, it used to be that you either had a kid, or you didn't, and that was that. Every time I hear about a famous middle-aged woman getting pregnant, I google how old she is. It's not about her body—it's because I wonder what at forty-six, or forty-seven, or forty-eight, made her go for it. And could whatever it is happen to me?

◆   ◆   ◆

I still keep a list of names I like for future kids. Now they're a little more playful, since the likelihood I'll use them is much smaller, but I do still have it, and in my phone instead of a notebook. It mainly functions as inspiration for what to christen the new cats, but also as a reminder that I don't need to stop thinking about it just because I'm passing advanced maternal age and into the perimenopausal unknown. And because names are fun.

Daphne
Gussie
Ina (love her)
June
Alberta (Bertie)
Marlease (Hi, Lizzie N.!)
Cassidy (appears in lots of Grateful Dead songs)

Kit

Minna

Whitney

Margot

Wren

Yetta

Crosby

Zeke

Gus

Albert

Woody

Archie

Levon

I would like to request that judgment regarding my name-taste be reserved for my close friends and family. For example: One night in Chicago, I went out to dinner with Ferial, Jess, and Dey,[2] and after a few—many—drinks we began talking about baby names. I know: Could we be any more cliché? After I revealed that I kept a list of my favorite names, the others were desperate to know what they were. When I finally revealed my top pick at the time—Levon— Dey scrunched up her face. Absolutely not. What?

I had no idea what her beef was. "Levon Helm is a guitar player!" I cried, probably waving a martini around. "The

---

2 Ferial Govashiri, former personal secretary to POTUS; Jessica Wright, former deputy assistant to the president and director of scheduling; Dey, aka, Danielle Crutchfield.

Band? Hello? It's also my favorite Elton John song? I listen to it every New Year's Day!"

Dey explained to me the pitfalls of the name Levon as she saw them. This is what friends are for. And maybe another indication that having a kid is still a very theoretical prospect for me.

Victory Over Big Panty

A few years ago, I was browsing Twitter (probably) and came across a quote from Kendall Jenner: "Every girl loves posing in her underwear." This was before I registered my every shift in mood on social media, but if I had been in the habit I might have replied, "LOL no they fucking don't." Maybe that's kind of an obvious statement—the musings of a supermodel on her body are obviously not going to apply to the rest of us. And she's likely wearing the most expensive and therefore least comfortable underwear money can buy. (Or that money could buy if she weren't being gifted it for free.)

But I have a particular thing about underwear, which seem designed by Satan himself to make women question the years of work they've put in coming to terms with their own bodies and style. We shouldn't have to put in *work* to feel OK about wearing undergarments, but that's beside the point.

The point is that I have a big butt.

I understand that it's not original or interesting for a

woman to feel self-conscious about her butt (or her boobs, or her nose, or her neck—hi, Nora), and also that the self-consciousness is a pointless exercise for any woman to be engaged in. There is nothing to be done about it, and I live a full life with my husband, cats, and job. I'm on a podcast! But I cop to the fact that I hate-watch garbage like *Bachelor in Paradise* partially because I like to sneer at the scantily clad contestants and tweet funny things about wanting to go on the show so I can disrupt it by wearing caftans and smoking weed. When I watch shows like that I picture myself as Waldorf and Statler, the two cantankerous old dudes who hung out in the balcony on *The Muppet Show*, mocking the frantic bodies below. I am not comparing myself to those women. I expect they all have gripes with underwear, too.

My first memory of a movie where underwear was discussed was *St. Elmo's Fire*, a film I loved as a teenager to the point that it made me want to go to Georgetown despite its depiction of Georgetown as an incubator for post-graduate confusion and delusion. Billy the Kid (Rob Lowe) is about to make out with Wendy (Mare Winningham) when he pushes up her skirt to reveal her prehistoric Spanx and says, "What the hell is this? This your scuba suit?"

Doesn't exactly inspire confidence in the cultural willingness to accept the female form in all its diversity. I used to think I hated the idea and ritual of wearing underwear because I wasn't "thin," that if I were thin underwear would not ride up, requiring covert adjustments in inopportune public situations, or dig into my inner thigh when for any reason—it's hot outside, I worked out, I had French fries for lunch—my body swelled a smidge during the day. I thought my problem with underwear was an "It's not you, it's me" thing. As if all underwear came in the same size.

But then about ten years ago I got the stomach flu and lost a few pounds. This is how all great epiphanies start. As soon as I stopped vomiting I went right out to buy new underwear, thinking things would all be different. I figured that if it was comfortable, as I assumed it would be, I'd have the perfect motivation to remain 135 pounds.

Ha-ha.

First, I tried Hanky Panky, which seemed to be in everyone's underwear drawer. Why are there underwear trends? I don't know. But just as today all the girls want to buy the "feminist" lingerie brands from Australia and New Zealand that seem to generate their entire customer bases from Instagram, in 2008 everyone wanted the underwear that Cindy Crawford and Julianne Moore wore. It makes a little sense considering that the Hanky Panky revival—like me, the brand has been around since the 1970s—coincided with the vogue for wearing your thong above the waistband of your pants. Imagine me rolling up to the White House with a bright pink lacy thing peeking out from my J.Crew skirt suit. I would have sent several senators to an early grave.

I took one look at the Hanky Pankys and walked out of Nordstrom. If your mom always told you to wear good underwear in case you're in an accident and they have to cut your clothes off you, where do Hanky Pankys come in? They make several styles, but the ones you had to get were the thongs or the "boy shorts," which are also basically thongs except that the part you have to wear up your butt all day is wider. If you rip your skirt, as I once did coming off Marine One, how does the Hanky Panky spare you any embarrassment? It doesn't. What's more, the claim that Hanky Pankys are "soooo comfortable" seems that it must be relative. Perhaps they are "soooo comfortable" for thongs. They say the constant-wedgie feeling goes away, but I will believe it when I feel it, and anyway I'm pretty sure thongs give you UTIs.

Next, I went to Victoria's Secret, to similar results. I had somehow never been in one; I managed to escape the enticing Free Panty! coupons they used to mail out. (Maybe they still do; I'm now happily past their demographic.) I took one lap and left immediately. Everything was so…complicated. I do not want to have to tie on my underwear. Trying things on also seemed unavoidable, and I wasn't about to spend ten minutes under dressing-room lighting trying to maneuver around all the superfluous straps, only to realize halfway through that the logic of the "sanitary strip" doesn't really make much sense. How sanitary can a thin piece of paper really be?

Next, Macy's. Something for everyone! Not really. Your choices there are "It's your wedding night…in 1987" and "Scrabble champion at the assisted living facility." When I finally did break down and try on a pair I was certain would be too big, they were too small. I am only 5 feet 2 inches—the idea of needing size-large underwear seemed to condemn me to a terrible and sad fate.

But they weren't terribly uncomfortable—no inexplicably tight waistband or scratchy stitching—so I bought a few pairs and cut out the size L tag. But then the stub of a tag irritated me endlessly. (This was before they started printing all the tag information directly onto the underwear, the way they do now. Advances in technology can really improve women's lives.)

It was unsustainable. So I admitted defeat and stopped wearing underwear.

At first, it felt like a dirty secret—and not a "dirty little secret," complete with dangerous sex kitten vibes, but just a little bit not allowed. I have no sex kitten vibes whatsoever. Or dangerous vibes, for that matter. But soon I found, actually, that it wasn't a defeat at all, but a victory over Big Panty. I should have been skipping skivvies all along. The reviled panty line was gone. I felt ten pounds lighter when I looked in the mirror. I came to the conclusion that the design of women's underwear is a patriarchal conspiracy to get us to hate ourselves.

Now, to logistics. I mentioned this in my first book, and earlier in this book, but I'll say it again here, too: The secret to successful commando is wearing a tampon even when you're not on your period. However, that didn't solve the problem of accidental exposure. While I worked in the White House, encountering a strong gust of wind while walking up the stairs of Air Force One could have been my undoing. So I channeled Wendy and went for the Spanx, which I determined after several mental calculations of pros and cons to be slightly preferable to normal underwear.

They compress your innards and you run the risk of constipation. It gives you a good idea of what the poor corset-wearing ladies of the previous centuries had to deal with. But in service of my country I succumbed. Though if our workday was inching past 7:00 PM and we were in the office, I did take them off in the bathroom, roll them into a ball, and stuff them in my bag.

When I left the White House, I vowed to never wear Spanx again. Occasionally I've had to break that vow. Same with underwear.

My secret was safe for years—until I made my first appearance on *Chelsea Lately!*, Chelsea Handler's Netflix show. I hadn't done a ton of TV by that point, and I'd never met her before, so I was a little nervous.

My friend Emily did PR for the show and was with me in the greenroom. I'd asked her to come so I would have a friendly face to pump me up before I went on, but soon she assumed a critical role. Everything was going fine until the sound guy came in to explain the mic I was going to have to use.

UM. 911. RED ALERT.

Because I had been a fucking genius and worn a dress (without underwear, yes) (to appear on television, yes) the mic would have to go down my back. In order to clip it onto my bra—which, despite having similar complaints about its design, is a garment I do have to wear—they would have to fully lift my dress, revealing my naked nether region, and clip it.

As the sound guy (respectfully) inched toward the hem of

my dress, I panicked, excused him, and got real with Emily. Like a true sister, she did what had to be done. I was mic'd and ready, with a little extra adrenaline to spare.

I don't remember how, exactly—maybe it was just on my mind and I couldn't help making a joke about it— but Chelsea said something about liking the suede yellow pumps I was wearing and I made a joke about my outfit that involved me disclosing that I wasn't wearing any underwear.

I felt no dirtier than I had before. And we've been good friends ever since.

But there's an epilogue to this story. Realizing, after that moment, that I couldn't free-ball it all the time, I knew I had to reach some kind of compromise. After kissing many frogs, I've found underwear I can live with: Gap stretch-cotton hipsters, size large. If they ever stop making them, I will use my experience from the Trump administration and organize a protest.[1]

---

1   As I finished up the draft of this chapter, I went online and bought ten more pairs, just in case.

How I Became a Crazy Cat Lady

For many years, I was not a cat lady. I was just a lady with a cat. A twenty-four-pound cat who charmed me and everyone who met him. And then somehow things escalated very quickly, and now I stand before you the owner of three rescue cats, which is about the max you can have in a New York City apartment without inviting daily complaints from the neighbors about the smell.

How did I get here? I didn't have pets growing up. We had a tabby cat, Buppy, who died when I was four, and we never had pets again. I always wanted one, but not in an intense way. When my schedule and life and finances were constantly in flux, I couldn't handle the responsibility.[1]

---

1   Here are some things to remember if you're considering getting a pet:
    (1) Pets aren't perfect (but they are purr-fect) (sorry): I am a firm believer in #adoptdontshop, and pets from breeders or pet shops are not guaranteed to be perfect or untroubled at all. Pets are like people; they can be unpredictable and nuts. If you want a pet but don't want to think about the possibility of puke in your shoes or training around "behavioral issues," maybe you should start with a fish. Fish can be cute.

Some of the times of your life when you can most use the comfort of a pet—college, the years immediately after—are the ones when you're least equipped to take care of one. For couples, getting a cat or dog is usually considered the trial period for baby-making for a reason—it's not as hard as having a baby, but it's not *not* hard, and it can be expensive. A surprise vet bill can drain your savings if you're not careful. You have to make sure it's fed at regular intervals, even if you'd rather spend the entirety of your weekend at bars and the apartments of various paramours. And even the most well-behaved animals can spring a surprise bodily function all over your new comforter if they get stressed or sick. Or eat beloved items of clothing.

I finally took the plunge in 2005, when I read a heart-breaking article about how all the dogs who were orphaned during Hurricane Katrina were finding new homes but nobody wanted the cats, who were being euthanized. Conservatives used to refer dismissively to "bleeding-heart

---

(2) Pets cost money: Before you run to the shelter, do a budget for food, a yearly vet visit, and the occasional pet sitter. If you want a dog but work long hours, a dog walker will be necessary, too. See where you net out and if it's comfortable for you. Pet insurance can be very helpful in case of emergencies and have reasonable monthly premiums. Once you do get your pet, start a savings account in case of a major catastrophe.

(3) Your life: If you have a job that requires a lot of travel, know that even if your pet hates cuddling and seems aloof or indifferent to you, he isn't. I used to know someone who would go away for two or three days at a time and do nothing for her cat but leave out water and dry food—no radio on, no TV, no visitors. And she wondered why she'd come home to cat shit in her shoes!

(4) Different breeds have different character traits: Do research on different breeds and what behaviors or traits are common to find the best match, and not just the breed that will look best on your Instagram.

liberals"—now it's "snowflakes"—and this is where my own bleeding heart is going to be on display: I couldn't bear to think that animals had survived such a tragedy only to be put to death. I ended up with a gigantic calico Persian named Tommy, whom I promptly rechristened Shrummie after the legendary political consultant Bob Shrum.

Because I hadn't had a pet since I was four years old, I was a little ill at ease the first few nights. I had a gigantic animal in my house. I could see only his tail swish by from bed and wondered if he would ever attack my face in my sleep.

This was an unfounded fear, as for the first few days he lived with me he hid under an old chair. I thought he hated me.

But with the help of cat whisperer Pete Rouse, he eventually came around. This was also about five months after I'd broken up with Doug, and although it's a little embarrassing to admit it, after I got Shrummie I was never so lonely again. We spent over ten years together, and his unfazed, stately demeanor charmed everyone I knew. Including DK, who used to live by a three-pronged philosophy that included the dictum "No pets."

Then, Shrummie got sick. DK and I spent a lot of time in animal hospitals, flitting around from doctor to doctor to find out why his legs were going numb. When Shrum communicated to us that it was his time to go a few years later, I was completely devastated.

I think almost everyone understands the joys of raising animals. Right? The internet's tendency to use cats and dogs as avatars for pure human emotion is indicative of that.

These dark political times call for heartwarming photos of tiny kittens nosing up to giant German shepherds. I don't have to explain why pets are good. Cats are better than dogs, obviously, but all are good.

But the thing about pets is that you're supposed to out-live them. They teach you how to love and eventually let go, to appreciate the time you have. They also teach you to have compassion for a life you can't understand, and for a life that needs you to keep going. (Of course, babies do that, too, but babies are tiny humans—we've all been babies, but we've never been kittens. A wild sentence, but I'm leaving it in. If I've learned anything in my life, it's that the line between nonsense and wisdom is very thin.) Before you have to care for something else, you're the center of your own universe, and I've only benefited from not being the center of my own universe. A good symbol of this is (hear me out) Instagram: People with pets take way fewer selfies, because let's be honest, a cat is much cuter than any human visage. At minimum having a cat in the frame is a good excuse to post a picture of yourself.

In the days after Shrum died, I hadn't yet learned these lessons. I thought I couldn't possibly get another cat ever again. Shrum was too important to my life, and he seemed irreplaceable.

That feeling lasted about three weeks, at which point I was emailing DK about a white Persian cat named Little Boy, who'd been rescued from a dog-hoarding situation. We took him home and renamed him Petey, after Pete Rouse, because despite the generosity of the rescue organization, it can't be denied that Little Boy was a really dumb name. Not least because he wasn't little at all.

He was terrified of everything. Me. DK. Doors. Windows. Food. Noise. Silence. My Birkenstocks, even though they do *not* smell bad. The only thing he wasn't scared of was the bathtub, which is where he took up residence. We couldn't get him out from behind there. So instead of leaving him there alone in the dark with his anxiety—which is not what I would want—every day when I got home from work, I'd bring his dinner and a glass of wine (for me) and sit with him on the bathroom floor while he ate. It took a few days, but eventually he was eating in front of the bathtub, and ultimately was eating like a truly acclimated Persian underneath the dining room table.

So a few months later, when we got an email from a rescue organization about a lovely white Persian named Bunny, I was tempted. I'd inquired about her when we got Petey but never heard back; now she was finally ready to be adopted. Actually, I was *very* tempted. But two cats? I had never seen myself as a person with two cats.

But Petey was doing so well. And it was Good Friday. Bunny on Easter? I had to do it.

So then I was a person with two cats. Bunny played a huge role in writing *Who Thought This Was a Good Idea?*, mainly by sitting on my computer and on Lauren's lap when she came over for writing sessions.

Then, a couple of years after we got her, she started breathing funny. This is something you have to expect with rescue animals: They've been through a lot, and you don't necessarily know how long you have with them. You just have to give them good lives and enjoy the time you have together.

I've spent a lot of time, energy, and money on medical care for my cats. If you're a childless person with pets, it's hard to explain with a straight face that you can't go out because your cat has lung cancer. And when it comes up somehow that you have covered your home in yoga mats so that your fifteen-year-old Persian, who is currently relearning to walk, doesn't slip, you feel your face get a little hot. You do these things seriously, because you care about the animals. But you also understand it seems ridiculous. It seems ridiculous while you're doing it, and it seems ridiculous while you explain it. Even many veterinarians will scoff at you. Bunny was eventually diagnosed with lung cancer, and when my cavalier vet called me to tell me, I burst into tears in my glass-walled office at A+E. The vet on the phone was, like, whatever. "She should see an oncologist in the coming weeks." In the coming weeks???? (We never saw that vet again.)

Most people can't afford or wouldn't think to get acupuncture for themselves, and here I am getting it for my cats. (For what it's worth, I've never gotten it for myself. Though it seemed to relax both Shrum and Bunny when they were sick. I think it really helped.) I wouldn't judge anyone who didn't get acupuncture for their pets or for themselves. But I understand I'm in the extremely lucky position to be able to do so. Why wouldn't I use my resources to help make their lives a little more comfortable?

While Bunny was going through chemo, I started working with a rescue organization that was housing several

Persians who had been neglected and severely abused. I promptly became obsessed with one who has an aggressive snaggletooth because some asshole kicked her and broke her jaw. She doesn't so much meow as grunt.

I knew in my gut that I was going to get her. I loved her from the moment I saw her. But I struggled with a lot of "Ugh—are people going to think I'm pathetic and collecting cats because I don't have kids? Is a third cat a bridge too far?"

There's no conclusion here except: Fuck that stupid train of thought. People live their lives differently. They can have different priorities. Mine is rescuing cats. I named snaggletooth Midge, because I had recently finished *The Marvelous Mrs. Maisel* and Midge is both a fighter and a hot-ass mess.

Bunny passed shortly after, so I could have been back at two cats. But then...well...we got Norman.[2] His face is remarkably square.

If I ever feel flashes of embarrassment, they're outweighed by moments when I see the formerly terrified Petey sitting contentedly on the windowsill watching the noisy construction workers below, or calmly not panicking during a thunderstorm, and I remember exactly why I love taking these cats in. Even if I can't save the world, or dethrone Trump through sheer will and angry tweets, I can make sure that a few animals live lives free of fear and full of human-grade salmon and catnip.

---

2 That this was also Jennifer Aniston's dog's name is pure coincidence. DK picked it!

CHELSEA HANDLER ON MY UNHEALTHY RELATIONSHIP TO CATS

Here is what you need to know about my relationship to Chelsea, besides the fact that within minutes of meeting her I was telling her I wasn't wearing underwear: She calls me Muppet, and I let her. For those who don't follow her Instagram as religiously as I, she's also an animal lover.

Chunky was your first pet. Why did you decide to adopt Chunk? And how did he get his name?

My friend told me I wasn't giving back to the community on our way back from a bachelorette weekend. When I asked her what I should do, she showed me a picture of Chunky on the website of the LA Pound. My mom called me Chunk, and I called my mom Chunk, so when I saw him standing in my office the day he came home from the pound, it was the first thing that popped into my head. Chunk.

Pets usually pass before we do. How do you cope? And how did Bert and Bernice fit into your life after Chunk and Tammy went to eat roasted turkey legs with Shrummie in the great beyond?

First of all, I'm sorry about Shrummie. You seem to have a very unhealthy relationship with cats, and I respect that. I can only cope with Tammy and Chunk being gone because

I have Bert and Bernice. Anytime you can replace a pet, do it. Why put off saving both your lives?

What's your favorite memory of Chunky?

I was paddle-boarding on the Hudson River in upstate New York, and I was pretty far away when I heard Chunk barking from the tree line. I was at least a half a mile up from where I had started, and he had been following through the trees the whole time. When I stopped, Chunk jumped in the river and swam the two hundred yards to my paddleboard. It took him almost fifteen minutes. I almost died of love that day.

What's the naughtiest thing one of your pups has ever done?

Naughtiest? They're pretty tame compared to me.

I sometimes feel self-conscious about having three cats and no kids—I assume people think I substitute pet children for human children. Do you ever have similar feelings? (Though having dogs is way more acceptable than being a cat lady.)

No, Alyssa.

Last one: Why dogs and not cats? (Be honest—I can handle it.)

Cats, for the most part, seem to be assholes.

Long May You Run (and Not Burst into Flames)

My first car was a silver 1982 Toyota Celica, which I inherited from my pop. It had no tape deck, some air-conditioning, windows that you had to crank, and when you turned on the headlights they would emerge from the hood in a way I associated with R2-D2. It was very futuristic.

In 1994, while I was away for my freshman year of college, it started dying. During the summer before my sophomore year at UVM, my dad agreed that if I continued to work my multiple jobs while interning for Bernie in Burlington, he would help me get a more reliable car. Part of the deal was that I had to do all the legwork, so I spent the summer in Rhinebeck reading the classifieds (like Craigslist but in the newspaper) looking for cars and visiting dealerships.

This was my first experience with car salesmen, who I quickly learned are a stereotype for a reason. The upselling, the pointing you in the direction of that beauty over there—it handles so smooth!—the blatant sexism. If a woman walks into a car dealership the salesmen assume they can manipulate her whimsical female brain into spending five thousand dollars more than she intended on random "features" like a touch screen that doesn't work and a Bluetooth stereo that doesn't connect. You have to come prepared, with facts and figures and with a steely resolve.

At first I just found really impractical cars—a banana-yellow 1970-something Mercedes station wagon, a really old Bronco. Then I found a red hatchback Saab, with tan interior, at Roberti Automotive. This felt like progress. Everyone at UVM had Saabs, and I wanted what all the kids had. It helped my case that this was the '90s, so the cool car was also not at all sexy and very safe in the snow and bad weather.

As soon as I got behind the wheel of the first Saab, I felt very comfortable. Among its absence of features, the Celica didn't have power steering, so you really had to put some muscle into driving, and since Saabs are like tanks, it felt familiar. Though it was a little less than perfect on the inside, I didn't care, because all the parts worked.

I knew I wasn't going to buy that day, so making myself out to be a shrewd customer who shops around (which I was, actually), I made a deal with the guys: If I bought a car from them, they'd give me five hundred dollars for my Celica. That was a lot of money considering that the air-conditioning hadn't worked for the last year and a half I had it and the muffler was always falling off. I made them put the agreement in writing, took the agreement with me, went home, and showed Pop. He was impressed! A few days later he drove the Celica over to Roberti in order to "check them out." A few hours later Pop pulled down the driveway in a royal-navy 1989 Saab 900S four-door! This was newer, and much nicer than the red one. It had heated seats!!!

I was beside myself. Pop said they tried to tell him the trade-in deal was specific only to the red Saab, but since they hadn't put that in writing, they did as they should have done and honored the deal for the blue Saab, too.

For six years, I took really good care of it, changed the oil, drove it like a careful and benevolent bus driver tasked with transporting small children to and from school every day. But one day it started smoking while I was driving it. And then there were some flames. Sometimes things just catch fire and you have to be prepared for that, even if the only way to prepare is by occasionally reminding yourself that sometimes things catch fire. I was driving down River Road in Rhinebeck, which is in the middle of the forest, so I have no idea how I contacted my parents to come and get me. It was pre–cell phone era. How did this happen?

Acknowledging the injustice of random combustion we face in life, my dad generously let me take his hideously ugly teal Corolla. I hated it because I thought it was uncool (I was about twenty-four at the time), but it had no miles on it and I didn't have to worry about it blowing up. It also needed almost no upkeep, which was great—I used to have to take the Saab to European car dealers, who imported parts from Sweden.

It was a good car. Then, early in the morning during the summer of 2004, on my way to work at the John Kerry for President office, I got stuck in traffic in front of Union

Station. I was really tired and really sick, so I sneezed. I hit the gas and rammed the Volvo in front of me, totaling the Corolla. The driver was really understanding because I looked as much of a wreck as the one I'd just caused.

It was time for me to buy my first car on my own. I had everything planned—I researched dealerships and models in my price range. Until I went to buy one and was told I had terrible credit because I'd used my Social Security number to sign up for a campaign credit card, which was used to charter planes and so had been hundreds of thousands of dollars delinquent for more than ninety days.[1] The moment someone tells you you've been denied something because of low credit is a mix of shame, panic, and dissociation. There must be some mistake! Indeed, there was a mistake—I made it. If only I could have used the chartered planes that my Social Security number had been on the hook for to get to work every day.

I left the used-car dealership near tears, found an old Saab online, test-drove it for approximately ten seconds, and bought it for $1,500. It was what I would call "an around-town car" because it was great to run errands in but not exactly a car I would take any distance on the highway. The farthest I would go was the Pentagon City Mall.[2]

This car was not in my life for long. It met its untimely end the day after Kerry lost. I'd been in Boston,

---

1   For more about this huge mistake, see *Who Thought This Was a Good Idea?*
2   Fun fact: The food court of the Pentagon City Mall is where the FBI picked up Monica Lewinsky for questioning in 1998 after Linda Tripp betrayed her. Monica was wearing gym clothes.

and when I got home to DC and saw my car parked on Fifth Street Southeast someone had smashed my headlights. The woman who'd done it left a nice note, very apologetic, and a phone number, which I called. When her voice mail informed me that she couldn't come to the phone because she was busy celebrating four more years of George Bush, I knew I would be paying for the new headlights myself.

They didn't make the headlights anymore. I learned that hunting them down in a parts shop would be prohibitively expensive—more than I paid for the car.

Because I had just lost my job—and because my credit was still "improving"—my dad gave me one more car, a green Saab, which lasted seven or eight more years. Until, spoiler alert: It also caught fire. You couldn't disarm the alarm, which would go off seemingly randomly in the middle of the night, triggered I guess by the ghosts of all my previous cars. But that I could deal with. The beginning of the end was when my battery died after I stopped for gas and couldn't turn the car back on once I'd filled the tank. The gas station guys said they could fix it, so I left it there. This was not a chain gas station, but some rinky-dink shop; I probably shouldn't have gotten gas there, but it seemed more convenient—and less awkward—than hiring a tow truck to take it somewhere else.

It was never the same again. One day on the way to the White House, it started smoking.

I loved that car. If that car could have lived forever, I would have been happy forever. But cars are like pets—you have to love them while you have them and be prepared to let them go when it's time.

You have one car catch fire, it's a funny story, just a thing that happened to you. Two, and you start to feel like it's a sign. Now out of the weeds of my credit score debacle—with the help of random garbage credit cards from Banana Republic, J.Crew, and Gap, which I always paid off in full every month—I decided it was time for me to get a nice car. I did all the research and thought: *BMW, yes. I'm half German, it makes sense.* OK. I informed all my confidants of this decision, and DK and Pfeiffer both offered to come with for the combined moral and masculine support. I was insistent: No way! I was doing it alone. I remembered my experience with the male car salesmen when I was younger and thought I was fully prepared to conquer them this time around. Get it in writing!

As soon as I stepped out of my momentarily not-smoking vehicle at the BMW dealership, I knew I'd made a mistake—I should have brought a dude. You can be as empowered as you want, but that doesn't stop men from treating you like a pretty little lady.[3] At BMW, this translated to long, hard-to-follow soliloquies on horsepower involving really big words. I'd come in thinking I just wanted to know about mileage and how it handles in the snow. But then I started to doubt myself. Maybe I *did* care about horsepower. Horsepower

---

3   These days, I can't recommend Girls Auto Clinic enough. Founded by Patrice Banks, GAC is an answer to all this sexism women face when dealing with cars, and they offer all kinds of resources on buying, repairing, and other services. Buy the *Glove Box Guide* and put it in your glove box!

seemed, to these men in suits, very important. But how could I buy a car with good horsepower if I didn't know what horsepower was?

I somehow managed to convey that I wanted to test-drive one. As soon as I turned the impossibly easy steering wheel to leave the lot I knew I couldn't drive a BMW. What was I thinking? Who did I think I was, a Kardashian? Do they even drive BMWs? Nobody needs a BMW when they're public servants. (Nobody *needs* one anyway. They're just very fun to drive.) They're expensive to fix, and I would look absurd.

The night before I had perused the internet for coupons and 0 percent APR-financing promises for all the car dealerships around the Jefferson Davis Highway and put them neatly in a folder: If you show up with, at minimum, all the stuff on the dealership's own website, the men working have to assume you're not a moron. I carefully drove over to the Ford dealership, and because my car started smoking on the way I took it as a sign that this was where we should part ways. If it had actually blown up, I wouldn't have gotten any money for it—and maybe I would not be here to tell this tale—but I was able to cool it down before I drove onto the lot and got $2,500.

As for what I replaced it with: I said I wanted something that could be fixed easily and that wasn't going to have obsolete headlights in three years. The guy was trying to sell me a black, end-of-season 2012 Ford Focus. (Always buy an end-of-season car. They're so much cheaper!) It had a tan leather interior and imagining myself cruising around in my sunglasses in it had less of a glam factor than the BMW, but it felt more right. "You look so good in this car!" the guy exclaimed, and although I knew he was trying to flatter me, he wasn't wrong.

But I had to stand my ground—I wouldn't be swayed by the first nice car salesman to tell me I looked cute. The problem was that this car was very "digital" and I didn't want screens—I just wanted buttons. Buttons don't short out or break. I was also convinced the sun would make a glare and I wouldn't be able to see what channel the radio was on.

Then he showed me a 2013 black Ford Escape. An SUV? I wasn't sure. But I drove it, and as a very short person, I found it pretty fun to be up so high. But it was more than I wanted to pay. I saw some other Ford Escapes a few rows away…and then I realized the salesman was trying to distract me from the two red 2012 Ford Escapes that cost five thousand dollars less than the black one.

Why were they less? Because they were red. We're not in 1986 anymore; red is not cool. Luckily, I am also not cool. I couldn't be swayed by appeals to vanity; I may have looked a little better in the black car, but a Ford Escape's a Ford Escape. I also opted out of all the new technology; I may have had to give up my BlackBerry, but I will keep the buttons on my dashboard until no one knows what a button is anymore. Throw in all my coupons and I ended up getting $8,500 off the sticker price.

I still have the car, covered in bumper stickers, and it lives upstate. My dad drives it a few times a week, and it's funny to think of him driving around broadcasting his love for the Grateful Dead, Pilgrim Surf + Supply, Walkway Over the Hudson, Bernie Sanders, John Kerry, the Wisconsin Badgers, Cooperstown, Bees, and organic food. I also have "Elect a Clown, Get a Circus," "Your Mythology Ends Where My Body Begins," "I HEART NY," and Friend of the Pod stickers. After more than twenty years I'm finally driving the SUV I wanted to drive in high school.

I paid it off when I was forty. (And called my parents when I sent the payment—you're never too old to be proud of being financially independent.) So far I've never had to have it fixed. Though I'm sure as soon as this book is published it'll blow up.

I Wanna Dance with Somebody (Specifically: Barack Obama and Jennifer Hudson)

You can't even look at a forty-eight-dollar candle or sample a new moisturizer these days without having someone lecture you about the importance of "self-care"—the idea that taking time for yourself is not frivolous or something to be ashamed of, but a necessary part of life. (The original concept, which was coined by the black lesbian writer and activist Audre Lorde, implied that self-care was a necessary part of a political practice, but today the meaning has gone a little slack.) Even if I find the constant discussion about it annoying—I don't think you need to justify every activity or behavior with some kind of grand philosophy about how it fits into your life; I love getting facials, but I would never say they're an essential part of my existence—I completely agree, both on a political and just a personal level, that self-care is so important. We need to take care of ourselves. However, sometimes we just can't. Especially when we're young.

Before my late thirties, I didn't have much control over my own schedule (or, for that matter, my finances). Trying to carve out the time to do things like get a pedicure, eat at a normal hour, or sleep past 8:00 AM one day felt more stressful than just omitting the possibility of leisure from my routine. A lot of the ways I unwind now—going to Pilates, binge-watching TV, having a long dinner with friends—were logistically off-limits when I worked in government. And once I started working in the White House, I couldn't even smoke weed.

If you think I'm being dramatic, here's a flashback to the 2004 New Hampshire primary: After spending the night—well, three and a half hours of the night—sleeping on someone's floor, I hopped in the shower at 4:00 AM and, in order to make sure I got in and out fast enough, held my breath the entire time. I don't deny that this is probably indicative of an unhealthy relationship to work, but if you hold your breath in the shower it prevents you from getting lulled into a steamy dissociative state and hanging out in there for who knows how long. Following a drive through about two feet of snow, usually you'd run into the entire comms team at Dunkin' Donuts on the way to the office at 6:00 AM. Since you'd last seen one another at, like, midnight, it was almost like you'd never parted. There was no time for a pedicure.

There was, however, always time for dancing.

Just as you can divide the world into cat people and dog people, I believe you can also divide the world into dancing people and karaoke people. (You could probably come up with all kinds of personality archetypes by combining the two, but that's a task for someone else.) Karaoke *can* be fun, but it requires precise conditions that are impossible to predict before you get into the room, and once you get into the room it's far too late to back out. Anyone who attends a karaoke party and doesn't sing anything risks being permanently identified as anti-social, suspect, and a party-ruiner. Even if you're game, there are just too many variables, too many things that can make the vibe take a hard right into awkward. When Gibbs left the White House, we had a karaoke party at a Japanese restaurant, and although Jen Psaki and I were initially enthused to take on a duet, our choice—"Proud Mary," the Ike and Tina Turner version—ended up being the longest fucking song on earth. (Who knew?)

The only saving grace of my performance—I will not speak for Jen, whose talents I deeply respect—was that I knew the dance because I'd seen Tina Turner in concert twice. But I'm not Tina Turner, and it was the singing, not the dancing, that made that painfully clear. It's much easier to convey a winning personality through bad dancing than it is through bad singing.

Since I was a very young child, I have been a dancing person, and when my parents signed me up for ballet and tap lessons at age five, my appreciation for it deepened. My philosophy was always that enthusiasm trumps skill, which is likely why my instructors always stuck me at the very end of the row for recitals—I always thought it was because I was short, but in retrospect the fact that I looked like (a really cute) Porky Pig in a ballet costume and was not much more graceful probably had something to do with it. I preferred tap—I love the move where you hop over your own foot—but I also understood that ballet was the foundation of dance, and it was pretty clear that all the tall and thin girls were more suited to it than me, a German-Italian meatball. I think my meatballishness probably helped me maintain my center of gravity during complicated tap bits, but still. I was never going to go pro. (But I MAY indeed take an adult tap class with some girlfriends in the very near future. I recently did a *Pod Save America* show at Radio City Music Hall, and during sound check an urge to put my clogs to good use came over me. Of course I indulged it, and my love of flinging myself around loudly came back immediately.)

I eventually abandoned dance classes during my self-conscious teenage years, so I didn't fully unfurl my dance freak flag until my intense work schedule left me no outlet for stress relief but something you could do for free at your desk, for as little time as you had. Think Abbi Jacobson dancing alone to "Edge of Glory" in her apartment, but, like, not necessarily on my own, and not naked, since naked dancing is not for me, especially in public. (Not that confident!) When I worked in my super-private ground-floor office in the West Wing—distant enough from the Oval Office to avoid bothering POTUS, or more likely, to avoid accusations that we were wasting time—my deputy, Jessica Wright, would come in around 5:00 PM and we'd put on music and dance. Back in the '80s and '90s, when music videos were more of a thing, my teachers would incorporate some of the moves from popular videos into our dances, and it was then that I developed my "Smooth Criminal" routine, which makes an appearance whenever that song comes on. I cannot be stopped. Crazy leaning-forward thing included. Pelvic thrusts included. Jess could probably accuse me of sexual harassment.[1]

◆　◆　◆

I was not the only dancer in the White House: I had kindred spirits in the Obamas themselves. As I keep repeating, working in the White House was very stressful. But that also meant the dance parties were off the hook.

What happened at these parties was meant to stay at these parties. Most of the attendees had very serious, important, public-facing personas. But everyone showed up in the spirit of the party, ready to dance and participate, because they usually took place after a big event or undertaking. (As in karaoke, participation is key.) The privilege of being invited meant you were assuming the responsibility of keeping your mouth shut about which White House senior staff member did a funky chicken that looked more like a funky emu. But I think the story of my performance at the after party for the 2012 inauguration deserves an

---

1 All dancing is not the same. Balls-to-the-wall moves require something with choreography, or hypothetical choreography, like Michael Jackson or "Bye, Bye, Bye." For in-the-zone, sitting-at-your-desk grooving, "How Will I Know?" is my go-to. Melancholic swaying to calm yourself down: Mandy Moore's cover of "Can We Still Be Friends." "Deal" by the Grateful Dead is for when I want to twirl around and pretend I'm in high school. ("The Grateful Dead, again???" I know. But just try it, you'll like it.) And then Led Zeppelin is for air guitar.

audience. I'm able to justify it because the funky emu in the story is me.

The conditions for this party to be awesome were there: It was the celebration at the end of an exhausting period of crises in addition to the election, and more importantly I was wearing a sparkly, sassy REDValentino dress (a gift from DK) that was short enough to allow me to get down, literally. There were also a lot of famous people at this party, and although you'd think that the presence of glamorous celebrities would make it difficult to let your hair down, they actually made you more comfortable. During the day, I always felt and lived like a government employee—broke, disheveled, huge bags under my eyes accentuating my J.Crew suit— but at these parties the famous people were pretty stoked to be around us. They didn't just love the Obamas—they expressed a genuine appreciation for what we did and how smart they assumed we were. Not saying we were. But we did do a good job. So it was always weirdly egalitarian.

Especially on the dance floor.

Over the course of a couple of hours, I'd had about three champagnes—enough to get a steady buzz and for my feet not to hurt. (Well, actually, most people had taken off their shoes by this point.) I do not remember the song, but I remember POTUS coming over to dance with a group of us. By that time, he'd made his appearance on *The Ellen Show* that gave him a reputation as a competent but perhaps a little practiced—cerebral, contained—dancer. But when nobody's around, he's good. Not as good as FLOTUS, but unlike me, who likes to leave it all on the dance floor, both of them exude a certain ease. They're not show-offs, but they're also not restraining themselves. They're just cool. I find, also, that the presence of famous people elevates the moves of everyone involved. You want to impress them. You want to be the government employee who exceeds expectations.

Back to the party. You know how you read stories about people in crises having superhuman strength? At this party I was dancing like I needed to lift a car off a crying baby. POTUS was always amused by my dancing; Pete Souza got a few fun snaps of him laughing at me while I danced to "Rockin' in the Free World" at an event with Eddie Vedder. As POTUS was dancing with our group, I became aware that all eyes were on us, so I began to kick it up a notch. I like to think that this is what started to draw a crowd. They weren't chanting "Go, white girl!" but if they had, I would have understood. At the resounding chorus of some song or another, POTUS began pointing to me and Jennifer Hudson. As in Oscar-winning actress and former *American Idol* contestant Jennifer Hudson. And then he kept pointing to us.

Keep in mind that the recollection of this event was formed by a drunk person. But I think what happened next can only be described as a dance-off. That is how I remember it anyway. My training copying Michael Jackson was deployed in ways I could not have expected. My hips were not lying. Nor was my back pain the next day. I got so low, so many times, that for the next two days I couldn't walk without the help of three Advil.

But I'm pretty sure I won.

Acknowledgments

I owe this book to all the women who keep fighting the fight on behalf of the sisterhood and who never less than persist. I also want to thank:

- Sean, Rachel, and Bob, for letting us tell more stories;
- LO. These books are as much yours as they are mine, even though you're a serious literary person and I still really love *Hello!* magazine;
- DK. You remain the best, and I love you very much. So do the fuzzy butts (especially when you let them sleep on your head);
- the people who keep me and the cats on track, answering my (sometimes loony, always thorough) emails, no matter how late at night: Dr. Goldberg, Dr. Quagliata, Dr. Hoch, Dr. Berg, and, mommy of my god-babies, Dr. Talarico.

Bunny Mastromonaco Krone
2008–2018
Rest in power, Queen

About the Authors

Alyssa Mastromonaco is the author of the *New York Times*–bestselling memoir *Who Thought This Was a Good Idea?* about her time working as the White House deputy chief of staff for operations for President Barack Obama. She's a contributor to Crooked Media, a co-host of the podcast *Hysteria*, and a lover of rescue cats (especially fluffy ones) and pinot noir. She lives with her husband in Manhattan and Columbia County, New York.

Lauren Oyler's writing has appeared in the *New York Times Magazine*, the *New York Times Book Review*, the *London Review of Books*, *Bookforum*, the *Baffler*, the *New Republic*, and elsewhere. She also co-authored Alyssa's first book, *Who Thought This Was a Good Idea?* She was born in West Virginia and lives in Brooklyn.